THE
LEAKYFUNNEL

HardBits had a strong reputation as an innovator in the supply of the plastic beads used by manufacturers for the production of a range of plastic products. This innovation had earned HardBits the right to command a premium, but this was changing as the beads became a commodity. Faced with the inevitable price pressure of a commodity market, HardBits' CEO Frank McInroth set out to gain Board support to purchase a small supplier with a premium product in the belief this would have a knock-on affect on their overall price positioning.

He not only lost his argument with the Board, but also his job. Frank's replacement Sue Hunt was hired, not for her leadership of technology, sales or operations, but because she knew how to be a customer.

The Leaky Funnel is the story of Sue's journey as she leads her team to uncover and then remove the roadblocks that prevent HardBits from earning new customers.

The metaphor of the funnel has been used by sales management for many years, yet the idea of a funnel that leaks is a twist - if an obvious one. Likewise, *The Leaky Funnel* draws on both established practice and genuine departure.

The Leaky Funnel is an extremely accessible story, which uses this story of discovery to reveal an innovative approach to planning, managing and benchmarking the Sales and Marketing functions as a co-ordinated resource. The false starts, dead ends, and genuine discovery are dealt with in an easy narrative style. Through Sue's clear-headed leadership, the reader is introduced to this innovative planning framework and the many useful management principles that support it.

THE
LEAKYFUNNEL

EARN MORE CUSTOMERS
BY ALIGNING SALES & MARKETING
TO THE WAY BUSINESSES BUY

HUGH**MACFARLANE**

Published by:

Bookman Media Pty Ltd
ABN 36 093 085 511
Level 9, Trak Centre, 443-449 Toorak Road
Toorak VIC 3142 Australia
Tel: +61 (3) 9826 1777   Fax: +61 (3) 9826 1744
Freecall in Australia: 1800 060 555
Freecall in New Zealand: 0800 444 333
Email: bookman@bookman.com.au
www.bookman.com.au

Grateful acknowledgement is made for permission to include the diagram and the related dialogue drawn from *Inside the Tornado: Marketing Strategies From Silicon Valley's Cutting Edge*. HarperCollins Publishers, Inc., New York, NY, USA, 1995. Included by permission of the author, Geoffrey Moore.

National Library of Australia Cataloguing-in-Publication entry:

Macfarlane, Hugh, 1962- .
The leaky funnel : earn more customers by aligning sales and marketing to the way businesses buy.

Bibliography.
ISBN 0 9751163 2 0

1. Marketing. 2. Marketing - Management. 3. Marketing - Decision making. 4. Consumer behavior. I. Title.

658.8

Cover and chapter design by PiXEL iNK MEDiA

Printed in Australia by McPherson's Printing Group

Contents

Be a customer...1
A beginning of sorts...11
    The bead queen...12
    Be a parcel 13
    An early clue..18
    Consultative sales...23
    Enough 27
Hearing voices..29
    Cicadas...30
    Marketing sucks 35
    Brand new brand news...40
    Don't do what you can't measure 44
    Building value..51
    The fish aren't biting..58
Four anchors 63
    Sales and Marketing are on different planets 71
    Buying process is ignored 75
    Tactics are arbitrary 80
    Our indicators tell us nothing..83
    Will it make the boat go faster? 86
Mosaic..93
    Chipping away 94
    A customer journey...98
    The funnel leaks 104
    As thick as thieves..110
    There's money in recycling 116
    The past reveals the future...122
    Anchors aweigh...127
The road and the rubber 133
    Strategy review..136
    Mind where you're sitting..152
    A common problem 162
    Parallel journey...172
    A model future 175
    Tactics 181
    Rhythm 189
Come Monday 193
Appendices 201
    1 - HardBits' plan for earning new customers................203
    2 - HardBits' key players 211
    3 - Sue's library 213

Acknowledgements

No idea is entirely original, and this work is no exception. Of what I present in this book, my consulting customers taught me one third, and their clients taught me another third. I thank both for their contribution, and for letting me learn with them; I have had the pleasure of working with some extraordinary people.

The remaining third was taught to me by some great people who share my belief that an idea is not valuable until it has been shared. Amongst this last group I include:

- Mary & Mike Molloy from TRB consulting who through their book *"The Buck Starts Here"*, and in some workshops I organised in 1997, first introduced (to me at least) the idea of a progressive, granular sales/marketing process that ought to be forecast and measured.
- Neil Rackham from Huthwaite Inc. who through his book *"SPIN Selling"* presents a clear, well-researched view of the process used by successful sales people to effect progression via discrete and pre-defined advances in the mind of a business buyer.
- Alice M Tybout and Brian Sternthal from Kellogg University who in *"Kellogg on Marketing"* strip the fluff from market positioning to leave a believable and usable core.

There are also many other great books used in the telling of this story, and these are duly acknowledged throughout and the key ones catalogued as an appendix.

Raw ideas have a value and excitement of their own. To whatever extent the ideas in this book have been proven though, I owe a debt of gratitude to the early adopters of the methodology which this book introduces, now known as Funnelogic™ (see www.mathmarketing.com).

In particular, I offer my deep personal thanks to John Ruthven of Computer Associates. At the time of writing, John is Managing Director of the Australian and New Zealand operations of Computer Associates, and he made an early and significant bet on the

MathMarketing™ methodology, and in the process he, and others in his organisation (especially Marketing Director Jim Fisher), helped to shape it.

Finally I must thank the many wonderful friends who offered their wisdom towards the creation and publication of this book. As with any author, I find myself wanting to thank more people than can be done. So I thank you all, particularly those who reviewed the many early drafts and provided insights and feedback.

Three colleagues from MathMarketing helped greatly. Jeff Reid for his strength and encouragement in harder times, and his absolute and constant insistence that I write this book. Paul Miles for his patient review of the first and last drafts, and unrelenting project management of the production of the book and of the Math-Marketing™ tools which allow users to operationalise the principals introduced in the book. And Peter Philpott for his cogent structural advice with building the argument and its articulation.

Belinda Castles provided highly practical editorial guidance and encouragement, particularly towards the end when, inevitably, the last 20% proved four times as challenging as the first 80%.

Any inconsistencies, omissions or errors that remain in the book are wholly my fault, and are despite the best efforts of these wonderful people.

I am also grateful to Rosemary and Jim for your guidance, Mary for your love and support, and Sophie and Cameron for your hope. Thank you especially for understanding that sharing knowledge is important to me, and for the sacrifices you made to allow me to complete this book.

Dedicated to:
    The customers who taught me, and then
    backed me to teach them a little in return.

Be a customer

Sue's was an unusual path. Conventional wisdom had it that there were three legitimate paths to becoming CEO of a company that manufactures and markets complex products:
- In the early development phases, the ideal leader brought technology leadership;
- In the growth phases, a strong sales or marketing leader was needed to accelerate growth;
- As the market matured, operational efficiencies became key and the leader was often drawn from law or accounting to bring a tight focus on costs and risk.

Sue Hunt wasn't hired as CEO for any of these reasons.

Sure, she had run successful businesses in previous roles and knew her way around the industry, but this wasn't it either. The Board had decided that their products were good enough, but that was all. In a mature market, customers now viewed the offerings from HardBits and all the other leading vendors as much the same. Despite being founded on leading technology, the market no longer valued this, and HardBits was going to need something other than technology to return it to profitability.

Sue was hired because she knew how to be a customer.

HardBits

Frank McInroth, Sue's predecessor at HardBits, was a strong leader, with a background in Sales. He knew what the customers wanted, and worked hard to make sure his company had the ability to meet their needs. He expected a premium for their product, and pushed his staff hard to earn it. As one of a number of providers of the plastic beads used by manufacturers as raw material to be melted and moulded into plastic for a range of goods, HardBits was finding it increasingly difficult to command a premium.

Frank's strategy was to buy a small company with innovative technology that could add to HardBits' range of products. He felt that this leadership in one small - but key - product would allow them to position as a premium provider for their whole range. He had in mind a small job-run manufacturer that was in trouble and could be picked up 'for a song.'

If Frank was mildly frustrated that more customers were not buying his products, traditionally known for their innovation and quality, then he was speechless at the thought that his Board would not help him to change that. Frank hatched a plan.

Every quarter, Frank and his Sales Director were in the habit of hosting a Customer Advisory Panel, which had become known as the 'CAP meeting.' Or, as some of Frank's staff had come to call it, the 'CAP in hand' meeting due to the frequency with which Frank found himself addressing some aspect of customer dissatisfaction.

Frank invited two of HardBits' Non-executive Directors to sit in on the upcoming CAP meeting. His aim was to gain support for his submission to the Board that they needed to invest in acquiring a small manufacturer. His argument was that the commoditisation of the plastic business meant an inevitable decline in prices and margins unless they created new products able to command a premium. This view had not enjoyed much support at the last Board meeting.

DHM was a medium sized toy manufacturer, and heavy user of plastics from HardBits. Knowing that the Manufacturing Director of DHM was generally friendly towards HardBits, Frank had asked him to give HardBits a friendly blast about being "just one of the pack" at the upcoming CAP meeting. Maybe even play it up a bit and threaten to "shop their business around."

CAP in hand

The usual suspects rolled into the meeting. Frank and his Sales Director had been careful about who they should invite to play an ongoing role in the CAP meetings to ensure it proved useful as a feedback and testing forum. Although one or another of the regular participants was occasionally unavailable, the meeting usually included the Manufacturing Directors from three large manufacturers (one of which was DHM), one small company known for its

innovation, one old fashioned manufacturer considered something
of a laggard, and one trouble maker.

The mix worked for them, and Frank knew that with DHM
primed to give them a friendly blast, the two Directors would get
the picture that change was needed.

The two Non-executive Directors Frank had invited to the
meeting were different as individuals, but had a healthy respect
for each other. Justin Armitage had a passion for leadership, and
liked to see a company take a stance – even a wrong one. Jenny
Guilford had been Sales Director for HardBits before retiring to
their Board, and that of two other companies. The CEO, Frank, had
identified Jenny as a natural ally on the Board. Given Justin's dis-
position towards strong leadership, Frank felt that Jenny and
Justin were ideal candidates to invite to the meeting to hear about
the product issues 'straight from the horse's mouth.'

But Frank didn't count on Sue.

As CEO of DHM, Sue Hunt knew that her technology partner-
ships were critical to her success. She had strong views about rela-
tionships, and decided that HardBits' quarterly CAP meeting was
a good opportunity to air them. Sue stood in for her Manufacturing Director at late notice, and neglected to tell Frank in advance.

As a toy manufacturer, DHM had made significant use of
HardBits' plastics over a number of years, and Sue had proved to
be a handful as a customer. It wasn't that she had unreasonable
expectations, but that poor salesmanship from the succession of
sales execs HardBits had thrown at her annoyed Sue to distraction.

"You guys don't seem to get it. Plastic is plastic these days. It's
how it gets used that makes it different. You have had four reps on
my account in the last three years, and not one of them has even
pretended to understand how my business works, let alone how
your products can help me win in my market. Plastix are all over
me with engineers and consultants, and if we hadn't had a bad run
with them a year ago, I'd have switched already."

Frank made an attempt to reinterpret Sue's words into a case
for differentiated product, but Sue would have none of it. She had

a bee in her bonnet about poor salesmanship, and made very clear that her issue had nothing to do with product.

"Take packaging. We shifted to metric containers for our raw materials four years ago, but you guys still use imperial. I have told each of the four reps you have assigned to me that I have to double-handle the beads to get them out of your containers and into ours. This simple issue adds a full day to our inventory cycle, yet you've done nothing about it. None of your reps have ever seen our inventory process, let alone tried to find a way to streamline it." Frank looked up as if to regain control, but Sue was just getting started.

"Your invoicing is inflexible. We receive goods from you many times a month, so we have agreed to pay 60 days from statement. Every time you send out a new rep, I tell him I want statements issued on the last day of the month. But every month, I get statements on the 15th. This means we have to do a manual cheque run every month just for HardBits.

"I don't need you to change your plastic beads, just the way you deal with me. Yet every time I get a new rep out here, they want to talk about new plastics and how great your technology is. I DON'T CARE! And I bet your new customers don't care either."

The two Non-executive Directors turned to each other and grimaced. HardBits' efforts to gain significant new customers were hardly the stuff of legends.

The CAP meeting was not Frank's finest hour.

A change, but no holiday

The inner-city restaurant Sue found herself in a fortnight later was not one she'd been in before, but knew its reputation as a place where serious business was discussed. it's the décor was not going to win any design prizes, but Sue guessed that many had taken advantage of its maze-like layout for discrete conversations.

She turned her attention to her hosts. "I'm delighted to see you again, but am not sure why we're here." Sue swirled the wine in her glass as she formed her words, before settling on "I think I said my bit at the CAP meeting."

"Sue, we want to make a change, and we need your help. We recognise the need for our engagement with customers to improve, and we'd like to ask you to help us." Sue's hosts were the two Non-executive Directors who she had met at the CAP meeting a fort-night earlier - Justin Armitage and Jenny Guilford. Jenny looked up to see what reaction her statement would get from Sue.

"It's your problem, not mine Jenny, respectfully. Don't you think?"

"We'd like to make it your problem, Sue." Justin, the other di-rector, wasn't one for beating around the bush. "We'd like you to lead HardBits through its greatest challenge."

Frank, the incumbent CEO, lost his argument with the Board. Three months later and several dinner meetings between Sue and the HardBits Board, he also lost his job. Sue replaced Frank with a clear mandate from the Board: *in a maturing market, make us win through superior customer skills.*

Sue had taken some convincing that HardBits' Board really un-derstood what they were asking for. They liked the idea of being customer-centric, but she wondered if they were really ready. On more than one occasion during the discussions Sue had also won-dered whether she herself was ready.

The Chairman of HardBits, Lars Ingvorson liked his market, but was not happy with his place in it. In the final meeting before Sue's appointment, he laid out the challenge. "Let's be clear Sue, plastics manufacturing is not going to change. There is no technol-ogy advantage we can create or buy. Our customers though, are innovating all the time, well some are anyway. We will win by be-ing more fully-embedded in our customers' businesses." He paused, more for effect than for breath.

"I want you to make us the best at understanding the cus-tomer. Not just what they want, but also how they want."

"*And* by translating that understanding," chimed in Jenny, a fellow Director. "We are not a university. We have to learn how to create, *then use* this understanding to our advantage. Being nice to our customers is going to help, but it's not enough. We need to learn how to understand our customers better, and then to leverage this understanding as a means of gaining new customers – many new customers."

Author's note

This is the short story of Sue's journey as she uncovers and then removes the roadblocks which prevent HardBits from earning new customers. In the process, Sue discovers an approach to earning customers that turns traditional approaches to Sales and Marketing on their head.

HardBits, Sue, her colleagues and all the characters and companies in this story are wholly fictional. Each character has been created to communicate one of the dimensions of a process that aligns the interests of all the key contributors for a business that is trying to improve its ability to earn new business. Traditionally either Marketing or Sales takes responsibility for market planning, but we have found it to be more effective to bring Sales, Marketing, CEO, Finance and the product leaders (Manufacturing in the example of HardBits) together. To do this requires a framework that each can relate to.

I chose to use fiction, and therefore a story and a dialogue, to make what might otherwise be a dry argument more interesting. In doing so, I acknowledge a number of risks, including that of appearing to trivialise the subject and the extent to which this represents a genuine breakthrough in the way businesses plan their approach to sales and marketing. I trust that the resulting story allows you to recognise parallels between HardBits and your own business, and to take away the key messages, but also to enjoy the process.

Sue's journey is broken into five discrete stages, each representing a manageable block of reading. You may wish to divide your reading into the following:

1. *A beginning of sorts*, and *Hearing voices* together describe Sue's attempt to fix a problem that she doesn't quite understand, and then her attempt to understand the problem.
2. *Four anchors* is somewhat shorter, but is worth reading on its own as it defines the problems faced by many organisations as they seek to grow by attracting new clients.

3. In *Mosaic*, Sue and her colleagues uncover the answers, even though they don't quite line the pieces up in the right order.

4. *The road and the rubber* puts these answers to the test and in doing so shapes them more fully. The execution of the plan delivers measured results, and brings Sue's first journey to a close.

5. *Come Monday* is something of an epilogue and together with the copy of HardBits' plan can be included in this final block of reading.

Along the way you will meet some of Sue's team and three Non-executive Board members. I have appended a basic organisational chart to which you can refer to keep their roles clear.

Much of what Sue and her team discovers is initiated by discussions, misunderstandings or incomplete interpretation from some excellent management books one or another of them has read. Sue's booklist is also appended to this story, including a brief description of the key message Sue and her team take from each of the books.

Now, finally, what this book is not: Sue's journey, and that of her team, is a voyage of discovery. What I hope you take from this book is dissatisfaction with the status quo of how Sales and Marketing is planned, measured, and managed in your organisation, and some insights about a framework for changing this. *The Leaky Funnel* will not give you a recipe of prescriptive tactics, but a way to select your own.

A beginning of sorts

The bead queen

It had been three months full of surprises. The market had been telling HardBits that their products were no different from others, and that they therefore needed to adjust their price. Frank, the CEO, had sought to change this through an acquisition that would give them some much needed premium product. He lost the argument with the Board, and his job. More surprising still, he had lost it to the former CEO of a customer that complained about their sales approach, not their products.

Now, one of the kids was in charge of the lolly jar.

Sue reflected. In June she had been Sue Hunt, CEO of DHM, Toy Queen, featured in *Fortune* as a business leader of the future. On Monday it would be October and she would be Sue Hunt, maker of plastic beads, invisible. What on earth was she doing? *This had better be some challenge. Tomorrow morning, I'm hunting for the fun, and I'd better find it fast.*

Be a parcel

Sue couldn't wait for her official start date, and didn't. Hunting for fun, Sue decided to get her head around the company's processes by following an order the week before she started. *None of the staff know me yet, this should be easy.*

Sue liked the idea of being a parcel. She didn't recall where she had read it, but presumably it had been an original idea for someone, at sometime. Anyway, Sue now adopted it as her own. *This is an ideal way to see the things from the customer perspective that even customers don't get to see.*

It was convenient logic for Sue as she wanted to accelerate her learning and get to the issues quickly. She knew product availability was an issue for DHM and for others, so it was a good place to start. Sue donned civvies, and rang Graham Chase, head of Manufacturing and Operations at HardBits.

After some short banter, Sue explained the reasons for her call. "Graham, I know it's a bit cheesy, but I want to do something that I can only do this week and will never get a chance to do once I've started. I'd like to come in today and look around the delivery side of things. I don't want to make a fuss and don't want anyone to know who I am. Can I meet you for coffee mid-morning sometime and I'll explain?"

Operations

As she entered his office at 11, Graham smiled as he admired Sue's attempt to look normal. *As if staff wouldn't think something was going on*, he thought. Then, "Sue, you're welcome to look at everything and anything, at any time, but I can't help feeling this is a bad start - spying on staff like this."

"I was half expecting you to say that Graham. It's not about spying, but about understanding. I'll never get to meet staff as an equal, and get an honest look at that part of our businesses that I know customers are impacted by. If I don't understand it, how can I help improve it?"

"I'm happy to help you with the learning. It's a good idea, and the boys will never get to check out your legs again."

"Hey?" Sue was surprised.

"I'm just getting you ready Sue. It's pretty honest and close to home down there. This is the wrong bit to be looking to fix Sue, but your education will be fun to watch – on many fronts. Let me background you a bit first..."

Graham Chase was a rare bird. He was one of the very few founders who successfully made the transition from CEO to manager without holding any resentment. He was a proud man and knew his department well. As a key stakeholder, and head of Manufacturing and Operations, he remained on the Board, and had been as keen to get Sue into the company as CEO as his colleagues were.

"Operations is a pretty well-oiled machine. We get a bit of flack for dispatch and delivery, but I don't think it's justified. You'll form your own opinion, but this is not where things are broken.

"Look at our stats. We achieve 95% of deliveries within the period agreed in our contracts. Of the 5% that are not, roughly half are due to weather or traffic conditions that occasionally catch us out, and the other half are late changes from the customers. Our inventory holding costs are low because we manage Manufacturing around customer shipments rather than the other way around.

"Our customers don't generally manage their inventory as well as we do, and we are looking seriously to move into Vendor Managed Inventory. That is, we'll manage their inventory, on their premises if we need to, because we reckon we do it better than they do."

Sue kept her disbelief politely concealed. On many occasions she had seen statistics that painted a good picture by being selective in what they recorded and how they interpreted key variables like time.

Trucky's mate

"So, you're travelling with me for the rest of the day. Well, welcome aboard. She ain't pretty but she's mine." Sue hoped her host, Steve, was referring to his truck.

Sue took no time to move the conversation over to the idea of how customers would feel about HardBits managing their inventory.

"Manage theirs? Not bloody likely. I get an earful every day from the guys I deliver to all over town. Ask the receivers at our customers and you'll realise we're late almost every delivery."

Sue thought *I wish Graham could hear this.*

The drive across town was actually enjoyable. The truck was surprisingly comfortable, and Steve's dry sense of humour kept Sue entertained.

Steve was a big guy generally, and his size was somewhat exaggerated by a significant beer gut, which was probably the subject of the odd jibe about "many years' investment in an amber fluid" or some other clichéd comment. But he moved on and off the truck as if he weighed no more than Sue.

He made no effort to ask why Sue was with him, and she suspected Graham had either woven some story, or instructed Steve not to pry. Either way, it worked out OK.

"About time you were here." The issuer of this greeting was smaller than Steve, but looked like he could hold his own with someone twice Steve's size. "*Hard Case* has been all over me since yesterday. Where've you been?"

Steve clued Sue up. "*Hard Case* is Howard Chase, his boss, the dock manager. No relation to our Graham Chase. Nasty bastard. No-one likes him, not even his dog."

"When did you order Nugget?" asked Steve, leaning out of the window of his truck.

"Weeks ago, when stocks got low."

Steve turned to Sue. "That's what Graham doesn't hear. I get this everywhere I go. I usually get to where I am told to go on time, but I get this anyway. You just learn not to take any notice. It must be the same for DHM."

Sue stopped, then recovered. Graham had obviously told Steve that Sue was still at DHM. It might have been easier if Graham had told her, but no harm done.

When they returned, Sue rang Graham whilst Steve took a coffee break before the next delivery. "Can we meet around six tonight. I'll be done around then and it would be good to catch up. Oh, and can you get someone to pull together the order and shipment paperwork for EnviroPak? I went on a delivery to there just now and I'd like to check out a few things. Great, thanks Graham."

Steve's coffee break was a long one, and Sue had enough time to also ring an old friend she had met whilst at DHM. Mike was Manufacturing Director at EnviroPak, and Sue had tried unsuccessfully to poach him to take over Manufacturing at DHM. They had kept in touch and Sue enjoyed their occasional contact.

"Hi Mike, it's Sue Hunt. How are you? Guess where I am?" They chatted for a while before Sue got to her point. "Anyway, I was at your receipts dock this morning and got the impression HardBits is always delivering to you late. Is that your impression?"

"Sue, do you remember any of us raising this at the CAP meeting? No? Me either. Delivery is an issue all right, but the problem isn't getting the stuff, it is working out when we need it. HardBits are turning orders around inside two days which is about as good as any of them. But they can only deliver when we order, and I'm not convinced we know when we need it. So someone goes into a panic and places a priority order on HardBits, then screams if it doesn't turn up that same morning"

Later that day, Sue was still in her casual gear after having joined Steve on another four deliveries around town. Looking anything but elegant, she took a seat in Graham's office back at Hard-Bits. "Well, I think I learned enough today to last me a lifetime. But for the record, Steve was great. How did you go with that paper-work for EnviroPak?"

Sue scanned a half dozen customer documents and system-generated reports. "Well, Graham, you win. It was pretty much exactly as you said. The dock guy at EnviroPak made it sound as if we were the sloppiest supplier in the world, and were days late on an order placed weeks ago. And Steve said that was pretty normal. It turns out they ordered two days ago and we were on time.

"I'd like a briefing on your plans for Vendor Managed Inventory as soon as it is convenient. Sounds like I should sit down the front of the class until I can learn to listen to the teacher."

"Nothing ventured nothing gained, Sue. Let's talk about VMI Monday." Then, seeing a puzzled expression on Sue's face, he quickly added, "Oh, sorry, Vendor Managed Inventory."

Sue headed home for a shower. On the way home, she con-soled herself with the thought that her day out had given her an early insight into why Vendor Managed Inventory might provide a simple and effective way to become more relevant to their custom-ers' business.

As she looked into the mirror whilst preparing for bed that night, she continued the dialogue with herself. *Surely the benefits of solving inventory issues would more than over-ride any minor cost pre-mium? On-time delivery is a real customer issue, and the key to solving that is on-time ordering. I'll need details on how VMI would solve that, and I'll need broad support that this really would be an advantage in the market.*

Sleep came quickly for the trucky's mate.

An early clue

Sue's first official day went quickly, even faster than her day of spying had. Graham had taken a two hour slab of time in the afternoon for a briefing on Vendor Managed Inventory.

It quickly became clear that getting deeper into customer businesses was going to involve change that impacted everyone: Sales, Marketing, and Finance would be as affected as Manufacturing and Operations.

I'll need broad buy-in Sue reminded herself.

Sue knew she had Graham's support, or more correctly, she supported Graham, but felt she needed the rest of the team on board. It was too early for Sue to start imposing solutions, so she needed this to feel that it was their idea, not hers.

She called a two-hour meeting to explore options.

From:	Sue Hunt
Sent:	Monday, 1 October
To:	Graham Chase
	Brett Marsden
	Kyle Hoffman
	Warren Jackson
Subject:	Adding value to customers

As you know, my first priority is for us to get closer to our customers. We need to solve more of their problems, and to be more relevant.

Our intention is to avoid price pressure from commoditisation. We will only avoid this if we find new ways to add significant value to our customers' businesses.

I'd like your initial thoughts on alternatives. I have asked Helen to schedule a two hour meeting, ideally for this week. Can I ask that you give this some initial thought prior to the meeting? No presentations necessary, just exploring your initial ideas at this stage.

Best, Sue

Sue reviewed the names listed at the top of her email to get a sense of how the meeting would play out. Graham she knew the best, and felt closest to. He was the founding CEO and remained a director. Brett was Sales Director and had seemed in their early meetings to not like sitting still. *Good.* Kyle as Marketing Director was out of an agency and clearly loved the creative side of Marketing. *Hmmm, not sure why he's here then. This is as dry as it gets.* Warren as CFO was pretty much out of the box. In fact, they all were. Stereotypical in their respective roles. *Interesting.*

On Wednesday morning, Sue's meeting with her team began on time at 8am . She kicked it off without any fanfare. "Clean sheet of paper. How can we best get deeper into the world of each of our customers? How can we add the most value and get paid for it?"

Sue decided to play a fairly unobtrusive facilitator role in this meeting. All ideas were good, but she felt confident that Graham would put up the most convincing argument. She was right.

Graham mounted a strong case for VMI, and had clearly done so before. He was fluent, compelling, and seemed to be covering old ground as the others nodded agreement almost before he had made each of his points.

Brett enthused about why embracing consultative selling (at significant sales training expense) would deliver the required change because each customer was different, and those differences would only be able to be extracted by a properly skilled sales person.

Kyle argued the need to reposition the brand and to change their advertising and collateral to persuade the market that Hard-Bits was closer to its customers than any other company. He also argued that research would be important. "Let's ask our customers what they want rather than have us make it up."

Warren offered the view that each customer's financial situation was different, and that they should tailor their contracts and terms around each customer, and move to online billing and payment.

How stereotypical can you get? Sue could not believe these guys were on the same team. One suggestion from each department, and each suggestion had no impact on other departments. *What happened to free thinking? This place is riddled with stove-pipes.* Sue wisely kept her own counsel. *I'll wake these guys up from their sleep some other time.*

"So, we have four suggestions, or five if we count Kyle's research. And I have two questions for you. Which of these would have the greatest positive impact on our customers and their preparedness to pay a premium, and which can we do most easily?" If Sue had expected debate, she was disappointed. As if rehearsed, one by one they lined up behind Graham's idea.

Naturally, Graham was asked to head the VMI project. Somewhat surprisingly though, Graham asked Sue if it would be OK for Warren to take it on instead. Graham felt he was too close to be objective, and this way it would appear to customers as a joint project between HardBits and them, rather than a sales and marketing initiative if it was led by the Chief Financial Officer. Sue agreed, and committed to give the project her full attention and support. Warren accepted the brief, and promised to measure it objectively.

Although Warren headed the project, all knew Sue was driving. The pilot customer, EnviroPak, staff, and suppliers all showed remarkable support. All embraced the change enthusiastically.

True to his word, on completion of the project some 11 weeks later, Warren assessed the impact against objective financial criteria. He concluded that changes under the VMI pilot such as holding stock at EnviroPak's warehouse and taking real-time feeds from their production systems had delivered little financial impact for either organisation. Graham argued that they had got closer to EnviroPak as per Sue's mission, but Sue wondered whether they would have got just as close to EnviroPak by sharing contract cleaners or paper suppliers! She felt that perhaps the benefit came from working together, not from Vendor Managed Inventory per se.

Sue and Graham reviewed the feedback from the pilot candidly over lunch. They agreed that the baby didn't have to be thrown out with the bath water, and that VMI probably remained a valid initiative. Graham agreed to work closely with Warren and with EnviroPak to incorporate the feedback and to redevelop their approach to ensure VMI delivered greater value to both organisations.

This was going to be a longer road than Sue had imagined, but she recommitted herself.

From:	Sue Hunt
Sent:	Monday, 17 December
To:	Graham Chase
	Brett Marsden
	Kyle Hoffman
	Warren Jackson
Subject:	Adding value to customers

From a list of candidate options, we chose to invest in Vendor Managed Inventory as an initiative to get closer to customers. We agreed this would have the greatest impact, and be the most easily realised of the options tabled.

Thanks to a great effort by the team headed by Warren, and the support from all concerned – even customers – the pilot project has provided clear feedback. Whilst there has not been any measurable impact from this pilot financially, there is no doubt that we got much closer to our customer.

We now need to refine the idea using this feedback, and Warren will ensure Graham gets all the feedback he needs to refine our approach.

Whilst this is going on, I want to explore other initiatives. I am hopeful that by now there is a great list of candidate suggestions to add to those that were tabled last time.

Please bring your ideas for change to me directly. I look forward to discussing any ideas with you as appropriate.

Best, Sue

Sue reflected. What had she achieved in her first three months? She'd learnt a bit, certainly, and had lent support to an initiative that was already in the wind, and would have happened whether she was there or not. *Am I on the right track?* The impact of this first mission had been modest.

Sue knew change always takes time, although she felt that her endeavours might appear to others to be a little aimless. Then she realised that they *were* aimless. Unfortunately, acknowledging this, and fixing it, were two separate problems.

Consultative sales

Brett passed Sue's office on the way to the lift later that day and stuck his head in briefly.

"Vendor Managed Inventory is going to have a major impact on customers and the way we sell to them. It needs a new style of selling; change is needed. I'm all over it Sue. Let's talk tomorrow and I'll fill you in. You'll like this, it's right up your alley." Sue wondered if Brett was like this with others also, as she'd found all conversations with Brett somewhat one-way and breathless.

"I've been researching the changes necessary, and have found the answer. What I want to do is reskill the sales force to embrace consultative sales, and selectively, enterprise sales. Neil Rackham describes this fully in his book *Rethinking the Sales Force* and I don't see any need to reinvent it, let's just do it."

"OK, why not come by some time soon and give me a proper brief?" Sue leaned towards the edge of her desk as much to avert Brett's gaze as to catch her PA's attention. Brett was a little more full-on than Sue was used to. "Helen, would you mind arranging something?"

Then, after Brett had hustled off, Helen came into Sue's office. "Brett does that."

"What?"

"Idée du jour. He gets all enthusiastic about something but moves on to new ideas all the time. I think he makes it up as he goes along." Helen hadn't shown this side of her personality to Sue before, and it caught her by surprise.

Sue wasn't clear how she should read Helen's comments or react to Brett's enthusiasm, and decided not to try. Not much was going to happen this side of Christmas anyway. She saw no reason for Helen to be uncomfortable with Brett, and wasn't happy with her own response to Brett's initiative. Maybe they all needed a break.

Deciding not to dwell on it, she dialled Brett's extension and left a message. "Brett, I want you to brief me when we return from the Christmas break on your plan for changing to consultative sales. And can you give Helen the details of that book you mentioned and any suggestions about where she might buy a copy locally?"

Sue's hunch was right; the two-week break did them all a great deal of good. Christmas and New Year were always a great time for family gatherings and generally getting an injection of good will, even for those for whom Christmas had no particular religious significance. And Sue had time over the break to come to grips with the essence of Rackham's book.

Although somewhat less impactful than *SPIN Selling* (Neil Rackham's first book), in *Rethinking the Sales Force* Rackham and De Vincentis pointed out that sales forces are often structured around conveniences for the vendor rather than the buying style of the customer. They offered a simple, usable framework to deal with the three types of buyer: *intrinsic* (their value comes from the product alone), *extrinsic* (their value comes from the way the product is applied), and *strategic* (they want to create new value by aligning their resources with yours).

The message was clear and Sue could see that as a minimum the approach would teach her sales people to respect that prospective customers had different buying styles, and that they should adjust their selling style to suit.

Brett was Sue's first meeting after the break. They chatted for a bit, then, "Brett, I have read *Rethinking the Sales Force*, and I get it. How much will it cost to reskill your whole team?"

"I've had a quote from a trainer we have used in the past, and they reckon $2000 per person if we organise them into groups."

"Do you really think this will work Brett? Do you see a re-turn?"

"Oh yeah, absolutely. We need to shift out of product flogging mode. Or, as Rackham would say, we need to get past the intrinsic value of the products."

She continued. "Good, I want firm costs, and I want to know what impact this will have on revenue. And you can attach a signed copy of your revised goal sheet to the cost submission."

Brett backed down quickly. "Well, it's not so much about addi-tional revenue as about a strategic advantage. It's not what my cus-tomers want, it's what *we* want." Brett definitely had his tail be-tween his legs, but Sue suspected he was only half committed to the training himself. The meeting apparently over, he got up to go.

"Hey, Brett, come back and sit down." She waited until he had before continuing. "Please don't come to me with a proposal be-cause you think it's what *I* want. If *you* don't support it, then don't advocate it. If you put an idea to me, I'm going to assume you be-lieve in it, and are prepared to defend your case.

"Of course we need to teach our sales people how to sell con-sultatively. *Of course* we'll do a few enterprise deals. You must make this change, but don't oversell it. This is a small step."

Sue went on to recount some of her experiences at DHM with sales people who had studiously ignored what DHM wanted, and how it bought. She had not previously covered much of this with Brett as she needed him on-side. Her outburst at the CAP meeting had not been raised by Brett, and he had not heard it mentioned again until now from Sue.

She had many more examples, but used just one to help Brett understand why she supported his push to reshape the focus of his sales people.

"Brett, the problem is not just *your* sales people. Plastix have a cheaper product, but very slick operations. Unfortunately, that slickness becomes decidedly slimy sometimes. Our last rep when I was at DHM had obviously been on lots of sales training courses – but not good ones. Every time I asked a question, he would answer 'so Sue, if we could address that would you be in a position to place an order today.' I hadn't even got my head around what I needed, let alone whether they had a solution. I got sucked in the first few times because they listened, but it turned out that even this was faked. It was a learned process and they had no interest in what I said. I don't even know if they kept their notes from our meetings – it was all just show.

"I came here to make HardBits the best of the plastics manufacturers at understanding customers. If this course is going to help that understanding, then I am all for it."

From:	Sue Hunt
Sent:	Wednesday 9 January
To:	Brett Marsden
Subject:	Consultative Selling

Brett,

I support your proposal to reskill your team to become more competent at consultative sales.

After you get everyone trained on consultative selling, I suggest you select your top 5 Managers and have them lead the enterprise deals because we need some grey hair on these larger deals.

I'll fund the training, and will not, on this occasion, expect a revenue budget increase.

Best, Sue

Sue realised what she had just written. She was now into her 4th month on the job, had a Board meeting in two days, and had still done little other than to entertain a few minor changes – no more than would have happened without her.

She felt very uneasy.

Enough

Friday 11 January was Sue's first Board meeting of the new year, although she had exchanged a few emails with some of the Directors. It was clear that these Directors read their briefing notes fully as they spent only a few minutes discussing the key indicators that Sue had imagined would consume the entire meeting.

Revenue was flat, as it had been for over twelve months. Costs were slightly up on this time last year, but not by much.

Sue had provided a short briefing on the two changes she had made. Consultative selling earned all of one paragraph in her report, and Vendor Managed Inventory consumed just a single page. The Directors questioned Sue and Graham to test their commitment to Vendor Managed Inventory. Then, once satisfied, moved on.

Lars, turned to Sue. "So how are you feeling?"

Sue had to admit she felt she had made minor changes only, and that her little foray into leading change had been somewhat half-baked. Sue suggested that she needed to dig much deeper into the business and to not initiate any further changes until she had the problems clearly in her sights. The Directors agreed, and the meeting concluded.

"Sue, a word?" Sue had not seen Jenny since her appointment.

"Listen, we didn't expect much to happen in the first six months, but I'm not sure we have made a dent. Nothing has broken whilst you have been in charge, but nothing much good has happened either. I want you to take a couple of days on your own to reflect. Graham can stand in for you for two days without impact. Take yourself out of town for the weekend and Monday /

Tuesday, and think about things from a different perspective. You're tweaking Sue. We need real change."

Sue didn't need to hear Jenny's comments twice. She realised she was driving in the rain without wipers. Until she could see the road, or at least the lights ahead, there was no point driving.

Hearing voices

Cicadas

Sue had already heard the Board's voices – loud and clear. Even the twilight screech of the cicadas at her holiday house hadn't drowned Jenny's words out of her mind. "You're tweaking, Sue. We need real change."

Sue spent most of her time walking and trying to regain the perspective that only distance from the problem can give. She knew Graham's and Brett's initial contributions had led to little, and that more aimlessness was inevitable unless something material changed.

Her holiday house was full of the inevitable pile of out of date magazines. Sue always enjoyed reading through these, enjoying the benefit of being able to look back at the journalistic prognostications to see how accurately they anticipated the effect of some change or announcement.

Sue mused to herself after reading one such article: *if he had known what the problem really was (or turned out to be), he might have predicted the chain of events a little better.*

Then it hit. The input she had gained from her team and her own ideas had all been about potential remedies, but the problems had not yet been identified, let alone defined. She had answers, but did she know what the question was?

I have lots of solutions, but I don't yet know what the problem is!

Sue knew from her own experience as a customer that one of the problems was their ignorance of customer need, but was a long way from seeing the causes. If she could get to the root causes, she knew that other problems stemming from these same causes were bound to present themselves. *We need first to understand the problems, then the solutions will come.*

On the Wednesday after her off-site think time, Sue reflected on her realisation that the problems were yet to be defined. For a moment she stared blankly out the window, then as the cogs slipped into place, got active. First, the phone. "Kyle, I need Sarah for a week. Can you spare her? Thanks, I'll explain later." Sarah was Kyle's Strategy and Planning Manager, and Sue needed some intellectual horsepower to work alongside her.

Sue's PA, Helen, was next on her list. "Helen, can you please clear my schedule from Monday week for the whole week, except for genuine emergencies? Get me a meeting with each of the people on this list." Sue pushed a piece of paper across her desk to Helen who was busy scribbling notes. "Send an email to each of them explaining what I want to discuss and why.

"Tell them I am interested in discussing their greatest fears and concerns. I want to know what's pissing them off."

Helen blushed as she tried to mentally restate the instruction, without losing any of Sue's clarity. The dramatic effect of "greatest fears" seemed somewhat at odds with the more basic second sentence, but Helen felt she knew exactly what Sue meant.

"I want to know what is stopping us from getting close to our customers, and why we aren't getting more new ones. I'll review the drafts of the emails and letter before they go out please."

Two days later, Sarah Martin sat where Helen had been earlier. At 30 she was still surprisingly green, having spent many years studying and not many working. She was bright though, and Kyle had briefed Sue that Sarah was a leading contributor to the Marketing team.

Sarah scanned Sue's list, together with her hand written notes:
- Brett Marsden – why aren't we getting more new customers?
- Kyle Hoffman – why aren't we getting more leads for the right kind of customers?

- Warren Jackson – why aren't we getting more out of each customer?
- Graham Chase – why aren't our products more useful to customers?
- Shane Watson of CliniCAL (one of our distributors) – why
  aren't you selling more?

"Sue, respectfully, there is one voice you don't have on your list,"
Sarah volunteered.

"Who?"

"Me. I have been thinking about this issue since you started,
and I have been doing some homework. I think you should see it.
Also," Sarah paused…

"Yes?"

"I think you have already proven that our products and processes aren't the issue. Why do you need Graham?"

Sue tapped her pen as she thought. Then, turning to face Sarah,
"OK, but I'll not be able to use you as an assistant for this week as I
had intended."

"Suits me fine Sue. I didn't study six years to get an undergrad
degree and an MBA to play secretary anyway."

"Ouch!"

"Sorry, I didn't mean it like that Sue." Sarah knew she had
over-played it. "What I meant to say is that I think I can offer you
more than mobile note taking. I'll be glad to brief you on your
meetings if that helps."

"It's OK Sarah. That wasn't what I had in mind when I asked
you to help. But I'm happy to hear your ideas. And yes, I'll get you
to brief me before the meetings. Leave it with me for now. I'll have
Helen set something up."

Sue and Helen worked on the email together later that afternoon, and Sue committed herself to a week of research. The memo
resembled nothing of Helen's initial attempt, as Sue had decided to
make it a personal, heart-felt appeal to her managers. Fortunately,
it didn't look anything like Sue's initial verbal brief to Helen either.

From:	Sue Hunt
Sent:	Friday, 18 January
To:	Brett Marsden Kyle Hoffman Warren Jackson Sarah Martin
CC:	Graham Chase
Subject:	Looking for problems

Team,

HardBits has earned a solid reputation for the quality of its plastics. Despite this, our products are enjoying none of the premium we used to earn from customers. The Board formed the view six months ago that we needed to become more relevant to our customers, and that was why I was hired.

You know this background. What you may not know is that I feel we have made little headway in that six months. Our attempts at change have not yielded much, and I am now clear about why this is so.

The changes we have embraced so far, as well as those we have on the table and are yet to embrace, are valid solutions. But they are only valid if we accept the convenient idea that it is not important to first know what problem we are setting out to solve. I do not accept that idea, and I hope that you elect to do likewise.

I have asked Helen to clear some considerable time for me to work with each of you, one on one. I want to conclude each of our sessions with a list of unsolved problems. I do not want to try to solve these problems at this time.

I expect your candour, and that you will give this enough thought beforehand to be clear when we meet. I want to know what you believe to be the main impediments that will stop us earning the right to serve more customers, and from gaining more revenue from our current customers.

Best, Sue

The letter to Shane Watson of CliniCAL was along the same lines.

Sue was impatient to get into this. She had expected to be well into implementing change by now, and was frustrated to be in discovery mode still. Even worse, she was in discovery mode *again*. But she felt strongly that until she had absolute clarity about the problem, how could she possibly know what solution would fit best?

Marketing sucks

Brett is such a bloke, Sue thought. *He wants to kill the problem, then it's all over and we can move on. I need him to tell me what is really not working, in his area and in others.*

Sue stopped playing with the gender stereotypes for now, but held to the view that getting Brett to let her in on his world would not be easy.

King for a day. I'll take him into my confidence and let him be King for a day.

Sue pencilled a few notes for her meeting with Brett.

Brett:

Choose location well

Repeat the brief (tell me what's not working, not how to fix it

What MOST stops us from connecting with new customers?

"So tell me about Brett." Sue was not yet clear how she would get most value out of Sarah.

"He loves lunches. He has a customer over to the Atrium at least once a week. All totally legit, only customers and prospects, and just sees this as a part of the job.

"Best Sales Director we've ever had though. His customers love him, and it's not the lunches. He prides himself on managing

a team who know their product well and they look after their customers well, handling any issues as a part of the team.

"And don't think that they're soft because they're not. They can
pitch it better than any of their competitors. Their competitive
knowledge is great also and they are not afraid to close. They'd
rather get thrown out for trying than fail to try.

"Kyle thinks Brett's alright too, but I don't think the compli-
ment is returned. Brett reckons Kyle isn't much good except for
organising brochures and the annual customer Christmas party."

"You're quite the psychologist aren't you Sarah?" Sue now had
a good background, and it was more favourable than her own
views of Brett.

Sue's own experience as a customer had led her to believe
HardBits' sales people were anything but good. And if they were
so good, why had she had four reps in three years?

She had seen the aggressive closing in action, and agreed the
reps knew their product, but she had not seen any indication the
HardBits sales team knew her business, nor that they had any interest in learning.

Sue decided not to call Brett into her office, nor to go to his. The
Atrium was out because she suspected Brett would feel Sue was
trying to tell him something about his lunching strategy. Instead
they had a sandwich sitting on the beach wall watching the kite
surfers.

"Off the record Sue?"

"Don't be stupid Brett. I'm not a journalist; I'm your boss. You
can be frank with me because you need to be."

"Easy, Sue."

Brett was right; this wasn't quite the beginning she needed.
"Brett, I trust you to run the Sales function, you can trust me to
respect your candour, OK?"

Brett didn't need any more preamble. "Marketing sucks. My
guys can get meetings. They can qualify, can pitch great, write excellent props and generally aren't afraid to close – although we're

working on getting better at that. Some of the guys could improve and some won't make it.

"The real issue is that there are not enough leads. And our brand is not well enough recognised. Most of our new prospect meetings we have to get from cold calls, and that's not efficient. We get a few referrals, but mostly it's cold calls.

"Fix that, and we'll double our revenue. And you can put that one on my goal sheet, Sue." Brett's reference to the exchange over goaling before Christmas reminded them both that many new initiatives were 'strategic', in that they delivered some vague return which was not measurable. Quantifiable returns were always preferred.

Sue digested this for a minute, but didn't take it up. "Hey, Brett. Did you really believe that *Rethinking the Sales Force* stuff?"

"Yes I believe it, but I don't see it as a real driver for us. I'll do it because we need to make that sort of change anyway, but that's not what my customers want. If you want to read something much more penetrating to get to know my world, try Rackham's first book *SPIN Selling*. That was written in 1988, but it's still my bible. Nothing better has hit the streets since. It's based on observations of an obscene number of sales calls, and describes a very effective approach to the sales call that is nothing like what most people do.

"My sales process is critical and Marketing doesn't help. They are the ideas factory: neat new idea every day. Trinkets, ads and events, just the more they do the less we sell."

Sue attempted to reframe Brett's criticism into a problem she could deal with. "So, the problem is leads. Have you discussed this with Kyle?"

"Of course, but he thinks I'm a whinger. He produces leads from trade shows and buys lists, but that's not what I need.

"I need prospects who are ready to talk turkey. When they've got the money, I want to meet them. I keep telling him that's what I need, but he gives me rubbish. My guys don't even bother following up the leads he gives us because they are such garbage. They're not leads, they're names.

"I don't know what they do in Marketing, I swear. You could sack the lot and outsource the event management and the savings would go straight to the bottom line without a hiccup."

Sue's meeting with Brett continued, but didn't cover much new ground. It was clear to Sue that Brett saw things in black and white. She had to admit she enjoyed that quality in Brett. They covered the issue of the sales people becoming more relevant to their customers, but Brett repositioned this as 'a useful step, but no silver bullet.'

Sue had set out to get Brett comfortable so he could be frank and to discuss problems, not half baked solutions. She hadn't counted on him being quite so frank. *Is this good?* She remembered her sister's favourite saying: "Be careful what you wish for."

Getting Brett off site was a good strategy, but she was not sure she had the full picture. Brett was certainly true to the stereotype image Sue had of most good Sales Managers: there is only one problem and it's somebody else's, and there is only one solution and it's mine. Somehow though, this seemed a good start.

Sue let Brett return to the office alone. She headed straight to her favourite business bookshop, bought a copy of *SPIN Selling* and settled in at home with a glass of shiraz and her mobile phone turned off. When she emerged bleary-eyed from her study at 2am, she wondered why she hadn't come across this gem before.

SPIN Selling drew on over 35,000 interviews with sales people, or observations of them in the field, and concluded that good sales people ask their prospects lots of questions designed to heighten the prospect's awareness of their problems. Then they ask more questions designed to have the prospects clarify their needs and identify a potential payoff for meeting these needs. Poor sales people ask too many 'situational' questions (how many staff do you have) rather than problem questions, then pitch products. The acronym SPIN comes from the different types of questions and the correct order Rackham proposes for sales calls:

– Situation (but only ask as many as you really need)
– Problem (to gain agreement to an assumed problem)

- Implication (to understand who is affected and how) and
- Need/Payoff (to understand what the prospect sees as the benefit of removing the problems).

SPIN Selling dealt substantially with the actual sales call, rather than the broader sales process, but thoroughly disproved the well-established sales management maxims of teaching sales people to "close early and often", and to talk about "Feature, Advantage, Benefit", which was a pitching technique.

Sue could see why Brett's team was good at wrestling customers to the ground, and perhaps Brett was right. Perhaps they just needed to feed the beast more food.

Her final thought before the dark engulfed her was a question that would have to wait until tomorrow: *Is generating leads a Sales responsibility or should Marketing do this?*

Brand new brand news

Kyle got right to the point. "Sue, I've been with HardBits for three years now, and we've accommodated a lot of change. Now we want to be a closer partner with our customers. The key is going to be to incorporate this change into the current perceptions the market holds about us, rather than trying to start from scratch. We have lots of brand equity already, and we have to leverage it."

Sue glanced at Kyle's desk. A copy of *A New Brand World* sat neatly on top of a pile of books, magazines and papers, its cover flap folded neatly into the last chapter. Kyle was an avid reader. "So, what did you get out of that?" she asked, pointing to the book. "I hear he was behind much of the branding success of Starbucks and Nike." The 'he' Sue was referring to was Scott Bedbury who as marketing executive at each of these companies had helped them to become brand leaders.

"He's a legend Sue. Personally though, for my money, Ries and Trout broke the real ground in *Positioning: The Battle For Your Mind*. What we are talking about is repositioning HardBits as a partner to manufacturers."

Sue looked at the prep notes, she had made the night before.

Kyle:

His office – his world

— Who is buying?

— How many more of them?

— Who is not and Why?

Sue recalled her briefing from Sarah: "Kyle is my boss, Sue, so I'm not sure I can be as candid as you need."

Sue hadn't meant this. "I'm not looking for you to talk out of school. Just help me get the most out of the conversation."

Sarah quickly got over her concern. "OK, Sue. Just listen to him. If you get too pointed in your questions he'll clam up and just tell you what you ask him. If you let him have a little room, he'll open up. He's wonderfully creative and he's identified most of our most successful campaigns in the middle of a sentence."

With a jolt, Sue returned to the meeting with Kyle. *How long have I been lost in thought?* she wondered. "Sorry Kyle, I was thinking ahead."

"What, about the next dot point on your meeting notes?" Kyle glanced up from Sue's prep notes.

Sue blushed, needlessly, before allowing Kyle to continue.

"Look Sue, I know why you're here, we all do, and you have my absolute support and can count on it from all your staff. 100% OK? I think we're all in the same boat, but we have different roles. Mine is to create an environment in which things can happen.

"Can we dispense with the foreplay? You asked us to prepare for a discussion about what is stopping us from getting close to our customers, and I know what bit I can fix. Can we just jump to that?"

Sue welcomed Kyle's directness. He continued. "Right now we are known as an innovator. The problem is two-fold:

1 – we are not really that, and

2 – they don't really want that.

"What we need to do is work out what they think we are today (call that A), and what they want from a partner (call that B), and then work out how to move from A to B. We are positioned wrongly, and need to communicate our point of difference more clearly."

"How?" Sue was following, but not clear on where this was going.

Kyle had a prepared answer. "I'll be the last to tell you what the campaign needs to look like, but I have some links back to my old agency, and their new Creative Director was on the team which did all the work for Scott Bedbury when he was at Starbucks. I want to brief them on some research for a repositioning campaign that will fit in to your new approach."

"Tell me more about who is buying, or at least enquiring." Sue hadn't forgotten her list.

Neither had Kyle. "The thing is, most of our customers are repeat buyers. When we want to get a new customer, we have to be visible to them at the right times. In terms of trying to characterise our customers, it's tough. There is not a lot in common between those who are buyers, nor between those who are not.

"The issue is: when a non-customer wakes up one morning and decides they are in the market for a new supplier, we have to be top of mind. To do that, we advertise heavily in the trade magazines, have a good stand at the annual industry gab fest, and run some PR, although mainly in the financial press – plastic beads aren't that exciting to the other journalists.

"The market is big enough for us to grow by 50% and still not have to cause any major industry adjustment. At 10% share, another 5% is not going to come by crash tackling a competitor, but by repositioning with the market to be the vendor of choice."

"And how will that create more leads?" Sue was persistent.

"You've been talking to Brett too much. Look, I could hire a telemarketing team to create more leads, or even to set up meetings like Brett wants me to, but what does that say about us? I thought we were trying to position as a partner, not move even more into the commodity space with telesales."

After her meeting with Kyle, Sue returned to her office, cleared a few calls, then dialled Sarah's extension.

"Sarah, what is the latest on positioning? Has that gone anywhere in the last 25 years?"

"How do you mean?"

"Well, I read *Harvard Business Review* like you do, and I don't recall reading anything enlightening. Has the marketing industry stood still for a quarter of a century?"

"Uh, maybe. Truth is, I don't know. My MBA course was still teaching the same principles that were popular before I was born, but I can do some digging."

"Would you?"

From:	Sue Hunt
Sent:	Tuesday 29 January
To:	Kyle Hoffman
Subject:	Follow up

Kyle

Thanks for your time today. I've been thinking about what you said. I had been hoping to understand a bit more about who is buying and who is not and why, but decided to hear you out. I'm glad I did, as I got some great ideas.

I understand your point about repositioning, so why don't you go ahead with the research, but not briefing a new campaign yet. We're not ready.

Get the research to find out where we are positioned today versus our competition and what they want, but also find out more about who is not our customer and why. Consider if you want the research done by the agency or a pure research house.

But here's the biggie: I want you to find out more about how they buy. The processes, who they talk to, when, etc. Can we aim for end Feb?

Best, Sue

Sue's unease about positioning aside, she felt there was something in this. Although not sure what, she was confident it would emerge. Maybe more time, maybe the research, maybe another glass of red? Tomorrow morning's meeting was bound to be a little humourless - Warren was a numbers man.

Don't do what you can't measure

Sue dialled purposefully. She had Warren's extension on speed dial, but somehow felt more in control when she punched in the numbers. "Warren, hi it's Sue. You still right for 8.30? Great. Listen. Do this for me would you? Don't come over until 9. I want you to spend 30 minutes thinking about the dynamics between Brett and Kyle. You've been on the management team with them both, and both of their predecessors, and I want your insights into how they work together."

"Does *now* suit?"

"Uh, sure Warren, but was I just talking to myself?"

"No, but I don't need 30 minutes to think about that, I've been watching them for three years. Be over in a sec." Sue had barely hung up before Warren was in her office.

Sue greeted him as he helped himself to a seat. "So, tell me."

"It's not hard Sue, respectfully. They just don't get each other. Brett has no idea what Kyle does and Kyle thinks he knows every-thing Brett does but is no less ignorant. They are smart enough to keep it to themselves and out of the management meetings, but neither of them hears what the other says." After a pause, Warren added, "I think Brett respects Kyle."

"That's not what I've heard. I heard it was the other way around." Sue had no desire to air issues between senior personnel, but needed to understand Warren's point.

"Maybe, but in my opinion, how they get on isn't the issue. They get along fine as long as they can ignore each other until the next meeting. I don't recommend you try to fix it, just make sure they have clarity about their roles and they'll be fine. The issue is not what they are doing to each other, but what they are both do-ing."

"How do you mean?"

"Give me 30 minutes to clear a couple of messages and get a coffee and I'll be back at 9. I've got a mini presentation for you on what is wrong. It's about time you asked. You want a coffee too? You'll need it, I've got 30 pages of detail on this."

After Cyclone Warren had left, Sue picked up the phone. "Sarah, no need for a briefing on Warren – I think I'm right from here."

Warren returned with coffees and a printed copy of his presen-tation. It was 2 pages long. Each page had a single point of just six words in 48 point type.

Sue smiled. "I thought you said 30 pages."

"Sorry Sue, bit of accountant humour. We have a rep for being lost in the detail."

This was going to be fun. "OK Warren. What *aren't* they do-ing?" Sue's focus followed Warren's as he pointed to his first slide.

Don't do what you can't measure

"Nearly everything Sales does, and absolutely *everything* Marketing does is not measured properly. We don't know how many calls Brett's guys are making, and we don't know what their close rates are."

Sue had heard the case for measurement before. "So what would we do if we did know how many calls they were making?"

"That's just the point Sue. If we did know how many calls they were making, we wouldn't know whether to be overjoyed or deeply depressed. Same goes for Marketing. They can tell you how many mailers they send out to get how many 'bums on seats' at a presentation, but nothing else that they do is measured. And absolutely nothing is benchmarked." Warren shuffled the second page to the top.

Don't measure what you can't change

And then stabbed the page with his finger. "There is just one exception to my previous point: The sales team is managed regularly to their sales forecast. Brett manages his Sales Managers that way, and they manage their reps that way."

"So that's good isn't it? I review those with Brett regularly."

"No. This is why I say not to bother measuring something you can't change." As Warren became animated his reputation as a dry accountant became hard to reconcile. "The forecast is too late. The sales team only forecasts opportunities that they think they've got a good chance of closing. If Brett came to you tomorrow with a forecast that said we'd not make our March quarter numbers, what would you do?"

"Task him with fixing it." Sue wasn't clear where Warren was going.

"Right, and I'll tell you now what would happen - zip. I've seen him do it every quarter. You might task him with fixing it and he might agree, but guess what? We won't make the March quarter. By the time the forecast looks shaky, it's too late to get any new prospects. Our sales cycle is about six months. We need to know *today* if June is looking shaky – let along March - but the forecast only tracks the ones close to closing.

"They even get goaled on pipeline – how many potential deals they have in the forecast. But this has no impact either for the same reason. It's too late once it's short."   .

Warren was right. But he was also wrong. Warren had only ever worked for HardBits and had no comparison against which to make his criticisms. Sales forecasts were a proven management tool, and Sue was confident none of her peers benchmarked sales and marketing processes.

Why did Sue feel so strongly that she needed to defend Brett and Kyle from Warren? Was she happy with their measurement, or was she thinking that because everyone else got it wrong, it was OK if they did also?

From:	Sue Hunt
Sent:	Wednesday 30 January
To:	Warren Jackson
Subject:	Follow up

Warren

Thanks for the insights today. You got me thinking about measurement, but I'm not keen to let go of the notion that Sales and Marketing should be more aligned.

I want you to do some homework for me, and I need the answers by the end of Feb. It's not directly in your space, but you raised the issue, plus you'll be impartial.

I need you to talk to a half dozen or so of your peers inside our industry, and another half dozen from other manufacturers. Buy them all a fancy lunch if you need to.

Two simple questions:

- 1 What evidence is there of Marketing and Sales working together? and

- 2 What examples are there of using measurement of the sales and marketing processes effectively?

Let me know if you run into strife. I don't want to hit end Feb and find out we struck a blank. Please confirm.

Best, Sue

From: Warren Jackson

Sent: Wednesday 30 January

To: Sue Hunt

Subject: Re: Follow up

No problems, Sue.

I'll get you the answers by end Feb, and if I needed to offer a long lunch to pull a meeting I'd be running Sales, not Finance.

Warren

Sue had underestimated Warren. She still didn't know where this was going, but she allowed herself to feel that the momentum was positive. Tomorrow was Sarah. She was learning to like Sarah and if tomorrow was as productive as the last two days Sue was in for a treat.

Building value

Sarah was undoubtedly bright. She had a tendency to be a bit academic, but hated being told so. She was well read, and had her head around a myriad of useful planning tools and concepts, and all the data around the plastics industry's competitive landscape.

Sue had learned to give Sarah enough scope to explore new frameworks and ways of thinking, but to closely moderate which ones she then put into effect. It was inefficient to let Sarah explore so many ideas when only one in four ended up being useful, but Sue had learned that the one idea which made sense, made so much sense that this was an inefficiency Sue was prepared to wear.

Kyle, Sarah's boss, liked the idea of having a smart analyst / strategist on the team, but had a less clear view of Sarah's worth than Sue did. Sue wondered whether Kyle's motivation in hiring and retaining Sarah was a little cynical. Perhaps Kyle used Sarah to broaden his colleagues' view of Marketing's contribution overall as a means of taking the pressure off Kyle's personal focus on the more creative aspects of marketing.

As had become her habit, Sue prepared a meeting note to ensure she got value from the meeting. Sue was no interviewer and was not interested in detailed questions, but liked to have around three points of discussion that would be covered no matter how wide-ranging the conversation.

> Sarah:
>
> How do we get closer to our customers?
>
> What do we know about the buying process?
>
> Who is buying and who is not?

Sue's office had a small meeting room attached to it, and Sue knew that Sarah would come prepared for a structured presentation, not a ranging conversation. This would be ideal.

Sue wandered into her meeting room to prepare her thoughts, only to find Sarah had already been there. The projector had been arranged in the middle of the table to point to the now blank wall. The framed photograph of one of their plants had been removed, and was now on the carpet leaning against the wall.

Sue felt a little intruded upon, but checked herself. She was determined to hear Sarah out, but marked her three questions on the adjacent whiteboard so Sarah would be clear of Sue's intent.

"Hi Sarah, come in."

Sarah glanced at the whiteboard. "That's not quite what I had prepared for Sue. Is that our agenda or a previous meeting?" *Pushy*, thought Sue.

"Relax Sarah, I want to hear your ideas, but you need to know what I need out of this discussion. Let's just see how it goes shall we?"

"OK, a bit of theory first Sue. You're familiar with Porter's five force model?" Sarah paused just long enough for Sue to nod before continuing. "Yeah, well the real story there is the three generic strategies. I'll come to that shortly. The five forces describe why one industry is generally more profitable than another.

"You probably remember that each of the forces (bargaining power of suppliers, threat of new entrants, bargaining power of the buyers, the threat of substitute products and rivalry amongst existing firms) shape how profitable an industry is. The greater any of the forces, the lower the profit that firms within that industry will earn, on average.

"Anyway, I believe the real key from *Competitive Strategies* is not so much why an industry has a certain average profit, but how you can generate profits *above* that average profit for the industry. Porter suggests there are three strategies to achieve above-average profits within any industry: 'cost leadership' (where you sell the product for about the same as others do, but it costs you less to make), 'differentiation' (where you make it for about the same cost, but sell it for more because customers place a high value on something about your product) and 'focus' (where you take one of those two approaches to a sub-set of the market). Porter argues that a firm must adopt one of these strategies, and only one, if they want to achieve profits above the average for their industry.

"As you know, we have a focus strategy." Sarah was moving between slides pretty fast. Each with complex diagrams and too much text.

"So, if we are using one of the three generic strategies, why are we earning below-industry profits?" Sue's question was as much to slow Sarah down as anything.

"Because we aren't executing well. A good strategy with average execution will always under-perform an average strategy executed well."

Sue had lost Sarah's thread. "Where are we going with this Sarah?"

"Alright, that's just the start, and is not my key point, just a context. If you buy the argument that any company can work to achieve above-average profits for its industry by adopting one of the three strategies, then the next question is how?

"The answer lies in breaking the business down into its major activities, and working out how value is affected (increased or decreased) with each activity. Porter calls these customer value chains.

"Now this is old stuff, but most analysts still hold this as true. Here's the clincher for us: if we can teach our reps to understand their customer's individual value chains, then we can work out how to add value and embed ourselves in their business processes."

Sue stopped Sarah, still not clear on her thrust. "So, you think we have to teach our reps to be strategy consultants?"

"No, it doesn't have to be the reps. They can sell the idea and we can employ separate analysts."

Hmmmm…

Sarah continued on, but had well and truly lost Sue's attention by the time she left to pursue her homework task.

The following morning, Sue was still reflecting on the change to the sales force implicit in Sarah's suggestion. There was something in the idea of understanding the customer's business, but they were a supplier of plastic beads to manufacturers. Sue doubted they could make the sort of transition necessary to pull this off.

A knock on the door interrupted her thoughts.

"Hi Sarah."

"About positioning. Remember, you asked me to look into this? I think I've found it." Sarah passed across a thick, academic looking book *Kellogg on Marketing*. Sue was still reeling from Sarah's dissertation on Porter and was not in the mood for more academic arguments. Sensing Sue's reaction, Sarah offered some comfort. "It's only one of the chapters, and I can sum it up for you now."

Sue drew breath and prepared herself for another academic lesson of only marginal use.

Sarah also drew breath, but to sustain her next offering. "If we are not positioned in the category, we should forget about branding. We can tell the market till we're blue in the face that we add more value, but if they don't know what box we fit in, we might as well save our time. 'More value than whom?' they'll ask.

"The key to positioning is:
1. Work out what the box is (in the mind of the target)

2. Get in it (in the mind of the target), and only after completely convincing the market that we are in *that* box:
3. Move to our preferred place within it"

Sarah tugged at her sleeves as if to pull them up so she could get her hands dirty. The effect was more mental than physical, as the cuffs on her shirt didn't budge. "Here is an example of a traditional positioning versus what Kellogg are saying. Volvo is positioned on safety. Ries (the original advocate of market positioning) argues you have to select a differentiating aspect like safety that is valued, and position in the minds of your target audience on this aspect. The problem is that most products don't enjoy the billions spent on positioning the Volvo brand, and don't have the history that Volvo does.

"Imagine if a new Korean car manufacturer came out today and positioned on 'economy.' If their ads said simply 'we are more economical', then people would say 'who are you more economical than? More economical than other cheap imports, or more economical than, say, Honda?'

"In our case, we are not well positioned with much of the market. The issue is we need to work out what general group of companies we want to be positioned with, and only when we are in that cluster, attempt to communicate how we are different from others within the cluster. We have to be *in* the group, before we can stand out from others in it."

This was better, thought Sue. "Have you shown this to Kyle?"

"No not yet, a friend showed it to me last night when you asked me to dig around. Why?"

"I think you had better. I'm fairly confident he hasn't seen this." Sue had been uncomfortable with Kyle's discussion on positioning and found this to be more grounded, more relevant.

Thoughts of value chains went out of Sue's mind immediately. *We're trying to build pyramids without laying a foundation. Too much detail on a base that's too flimsy.*

From: Sue Hunt

Sent: Thursday, 31 January

To: Sarah Martin

Subject: Follow up

Sarah

Thanks for your time today and for the homework you obviously did. I understand your views on how we can get closer to our customers. For now though, we need to park the value chain discussion. There is much that needs to be covered before we can make a call on that.

I need you to take on some tasks from today:

- 1 Porter's books are too long. Get me a summary of Porter's view on the three generic strategies, and argue which one we are following, why that is the most appropriate, and what we need to do to fully execute. Don't show it to me until you can get all this down to less than 500 words.

- 2 Summarise that Kellogg chapter down to a page or two, and work with Kyle on what box you think we are in. I have asked him to commission some customer research and we need to factor into that the notion of what boxes our customers use, which ones we are in, who else is in there, and where we all sit. We'll look at the research results and make a call on what to do going forward, I just want the homework done for now.

- 3 Do some research on buying processes. I want to know if there is a framework we should be using to understand the buying processes of our customers. We'll make up our own if we have to, but I want to know if there is some existing logic we should be using.

Thanks again Sarah,

Best, Sue

Bitter sweet. Sue felt she had gained a different insight than the one Sarah had intended. But that was OK, wasn't it? *Isn't this just another key piece of the puzzle?* Tomorrow was the last of her exploratory meetings and she still felt she hadn't got to the bottom of the customer issue.

Most of the insights were internal, or at least were about Hard-Bits' perspective. Sue hoped Shane would have something to contribute about the customers' world.

The fish aren't biting

Shane Watson ran CliniCAL, a specialist distributor for the healthcare manufacturers, and a HardBits customer. They had built a
business out of distributing a range of goods, which were considered non-strategic. That is, individually the goods were of little
importance to their customers, but collectively amounted to a fair
share of their annual budget.

Shane knew his market well. "Sue, we're in the business of
making ourselves absolutely critical for the unimportant to the un-
informed."

"Cute Shane, but what do you mean?"

"For the healthcare industry, there are a range of factors (key
raw materials, training, R&D, labour, Government regulation)
which they consider to be critical inputs. They are very good at
managing them, and you could say that almost all of my customers are in the business of outdoing each other in how well they
manage these factors.

"Then there are all the other factors. This is what we call 'non-
strategic' goods. These guys don't have high and low priorities,
they have extremes: super-high priorities and non-priorities. Anything not on the super-high priority list is automatically a non-
priority. For us, all *their* non-priorities are *our* high priorities. We
know their non-priorities as well as the healthcare companies
know their super-high priority list items. Without us, they'd never
have toilet paper or pens."

"So plastics are non-priorities?"

"Afraid so Sue. Get over it though, that's just your reality. Work
with the cards you're dealt, Sue. That's what we do."

Sue glanced at her prep notes.

Shane Watson:

— Why aren't customers buying more?

— Who are they buying from?

— Why?

Brett had told Sue that Shane sourced from multiple plastics suppliers, much as he did for his other products. HardBits had tried over the years to create bias, but Shane was a pure price buyer.

Shane's office was much as Sue had expected: functional, but not much more. Distributors typically managed their costs down, even though many of them drove Porsches to their beachside homes at night. The office was practical and so was Shane.

"How much of your plastics business do we enjoy Shane?" Sue knew she could be direct.

"About 30%. Seems to go up and down with your ability to offer realistic pricing, which you typically get better at towards the end of quarter when you're reps are a bit short on quota."

"So what would make you want to buy more from us?"

"Bring your prices back to reality, recognise you're a bit player in the chain, and give me basic product for a good price. I'm not being nasty and I'm not playing games with you Sue. Frank and Brett have come down here every quarter, and I tell them the same thing. You guys just don't like what I say, so you ignore me. Don't fret though Sue, your competitors are no better, that's why you still get 30%."

"What about your customers, what changes their propensity to buy?" Sue wasn't giving up without a fight.

"I think I've already told you that Sue. Your stuff is not critical to their business. They buy what they need when they realise they have forgotten to buy some."

"But couldn't we work together to help them realise what they could be doing with plastics?"

"What problem are you solving Sue? If they aren't hurting, they aren't buying. You can't make them hurt."

That was it, thought Sue as she drove back to the office. *We want to tell our customers why our products are superior. We assume they want to know that, but they don't. And then we have to wait until they have a need so we can sell them something.*

Nothing happens until they are hurting. So,

HardBits needs to become expert in identifying pain, and perhaps even creating it.

Sue realised Shane was not going to be persuaded. He was rather fond of his own view of the business. If she were to get more of Shane's business it would involve influencing his customers directly.

From: Sue Hunt

Sent: Friday, 1 February

To: Brett Marsden

Subject: CliniCAL

Brett

As you know, I met this morning with Shane Watson at CliniCAL. My intent was to find out why his customers aren't buying more, and why he wasn't selling our products ahead of others. I suspect Shane told me exactly what he has been telling you and Frank, and probably all of his suppliers, for years.

He gave me a clue though, and I'd like you to do some homework with your team over the next few weeks.

You are a great advocate of *SPIN Selling*, and I've seen behaviour from your sales people that suggests they are well-drilled.

Part of SPIN is identifying the problem. I want your guys to record every customer or prospect meeting for the next three weeks. I want them to record just two things: what problem do they have; and how clear are they in explaining that problem. I don't want to know what they are telling you they need, I only want to know why – that is, the problem.

I'd like your report by the end of Feb, or before if you have it. Give me a buzz if you see any issues with this.

Best, Sue

Monday was the Board meeting. Sue had half of Friday, and probably all of Saturday to prepare. She had requested a two-hour slot with the Board after the usual agenda items had been completed, and didn't yet have a single coherent thought. Before leaving for home on Friday night, Sue created a note to the team.

From:	Sue Hunt
Sent:	Friday, 1 February
To:	Brett Marsden
	Kyle Hoffman
	Warren Jackson
	Sarah Martin
CC:	Graham Chase
Subject:	Conclusions

Team,

Thanks for your time and perspective over the last week.

I learned some things I wasn't looking for, heard some of what you told me, and found little of what I was looking for. I am nonetheless satisfied. To explain:

– Brett has helped me understand the importance of keeping the sales force fed with quality leads;

– Kyle has argued the need to research our market and better understand their needs;

– Warren has explained the importance of measurement and focus;

– Sarah helped me understand positioning, and why we must be in the right frame of reference with our prospects; and

– One of our distributors put into perspective that not all of our customers would welcome a closer relationship.

I took more also from our meetings, but have yet to sift through it to gain clarity and perspective.

Best, Sue

Sue elected not to send the email. There was too much that remained unclear to share this with the team yet. The Board though, couldn't wait. It was going to be a busy weekend.

Four anchors

On Saturday morning, Sue went for a brisk early walk as she often did on days when she wasn't likely to get to the gym. Saturdays were always busy at the gym, so the walk was more common than not. She had a variety of favourite paths, but Saturday was usually down by the marina. It had been years since she had been actively involved in the sailing scene, but the movement of boats in the tide and wind still gave her a sense of perspective.

Although the sky was reasonably clear this morning, last night's storm had left the water quite lumpy. The smaller boats bobbed about like the hands of children trying to attract the attention of the teacher when they have been asked an easy question in class.

One of the larger yachts, *Four Seasons*, was anchored a few hundred metres from the marina. The short, choppy waves and the hull of the yacht both reflected the morning sun, and its size meant it had none of the impatience of the smaller boats. Whilst they bobbed about in the choppy water, the larger *Four Seasons* looked decidedly unaffected.

The effect of tide was another matter altogether. With her deep keel and ample hull, *Four Seasons* was pulling against her anchor chain in a most determined manner. The heavy gauge chain was easily up to the job, but the anchor itself must have earned its keep in the storm. Then Sue noticed that *Four Seasons* was secured not just by her normal anchor from the bow, but also by a second anchor on equally strong chain attached to the stern.

Sue remembered from her sailing days that often when boats were anchored close to each other, or if wind or tide was likely to bring the boats too close together, that this second anchor was often used to keep them apart. She recalled one such trip when the bow anchor had given way on the yacht they were all sleeping on, and they had spent the night secured only by their stern anchor. As the boat swung violently around without the benefit of the main anchor, the stern was smacked noisily by the oncoming waves.

After shifting the rear anchor to the bow again, they had decided that two of the crew would stay awake all night with the engine running in case this anchor also gave way and they needed to head out to sea. It had been a good lesson in safety for them all.

The lightning of last night was not evident this morning. Not in the sky, and not in Sue's mind - the wheels turned slowly. The realisation that she had just stumbled across an ideal framework for describing the problems to the Board came slowly, and without any fanfare. The framework that emerged did not add any insight to the problem per se, but it did provide a convenient way of grouping what had previously seemed to be a laundry list of issues.

Sue spent the balance of the weekend preparing for the Board meeting, and she retired early on Sunday night feeling she had some shape to her argument.

Monday 8am

Lars waited for his fellow Board members to settle before beginning.

"You have heard me say before that I would rather have all the Directors and the executive firmly committed to the wrong strategy, than only some of you committed to the right one. It goes without saying that it would be better still to have everyone committed to the right strategy. But don't lose the importance of my point, just because of its simplicity. We are in a mature, unyielding market, and must all be pulling in the same direction.

"Now, I have not personally been an advocate of this Vendor Managed Inventory strategy of yours Sue, but neither have I been against it. My interest was in seeing that it was fully looked at and that you had a clear plan for its execution. I am now satisfied on that front."

Sue went to interrupt him, but thought better of it. Vendor Managed Inventory was Graham's idea, not hers. But Lars' comments were starting to sound like an address, not a conversation. *Best to hear him out.*

"My view must always be that we back you or sack you. I prefer to back you, and I believe so do your other Directors. If you tell us you think you can get some leverage from VMI, and that you can be different, then I back you."

Sue felt suddenly very cold. She sensed Lars was building to something, and he was. He quietly passed around a photocopied clipping from this morning's financial papers. It seemed from the look on everyone's faces that he was the only one in the room who had had time to read the paper this morning. Instantly, they all regretted that.

Managed plastic?

In a move aimed at helping customers reduce their inventory holding costs, raw plastic supplier Plastix Inc, today moved to introduce a new service whereby they would manage customers' inventory on their behalf.

"Vendor Managed Inventory is not a new idea, but the benefits have yet to be realised by many manufacturers," said Brian Larthan, CEO of SureSlice, maker of plastic kitchen appliances. "We have been piloting the idea with Plastix for six months, and have reduced our holding costs by over 12 percent."

Analysts predict that Vendor Managed Inventory can lead to aggregate cost savings of over 20 percent, especially if adopted widely within an industry.

"Oh, crap." Graham was first. Jenny was silent. Justin looked like he had just had the air forcibly removed from his lungs. Lars, like Jenny, sat watching the others' reactions. Thinking, taking it in.

Although Lars was not the next to speak, he was the next to be heard. Everyone began talking at once and nothing of what any of them could be understood.

Lars stood up. It had the desired effect: the babble died away quickly.

"I want to hear from Sue." And then turning to face her, "Sue, what does this mean?"

Sue stood up decisively. She had prepared a strong presentation for the Board meeting, and her opening comments made even more sense now than they had on Sunday morning when she wrote them. Sue turned her attention to her fellow Directors, drew breath and began.

"When you invited me to join as CEO, you told me that you wanted me because I knew how to be a customer. You said that the one thing that would make us win going forward would be our ability to understand our customers. Your vision was that we embed ourselves in our customers' businesses, and leverage that deeper understanding.

"Graham has told me, and I now hold the same view, that there are no silver bullets. Vendor Managed Inventory is, respectfully, not the silver bullet either. It wasn't yesterday for us, and it isn't today for Plastix, or for us. We have implemented VMI with a few of our customers, and have had some positive results. But this has not been universal, and the change has not been dramatic."

Although she had their complete attention, Sue hadn't noticed. She was having one of those 'out of body' experiences one occasionally gets when delivering a critical presentation. Something like the 'runner's high' perhaps.

"Plastix have just made a complete mistake. VMI is an OK initiative, and I believe it will also be a part of our model of business going forward. But what they have just done is to send three messages to the market.

"One - those companies who want their inventory managed by their bead supplier have just been told there is one company who will now do it.

"Two - the other 98% of companies, who don't **yet** believe they want to have their inventory managed, have just been told that one of their suppliers thinks they can do it better than them.

"The third message is to signal their intentions to us and the others in the industry. For us, nothing has changed."

Sue drew breath before continuing. "Today, I asked for a solid slot on the agenda to tell you what I have learned. I had a couple of false starts early on, and set out, subsequently, to find out what was wrong before looking for a remedy.

"We have four problems, and although I can't tell you today how I plan to fix them, I will tell you this: the answer to these problems will probably not require discussion in this forum. I suspect that the problems we have are going to be solved by remarkably minor changes. The good news is I believe our competitors are not getting these right either. If we get them right though, the impact will be significant.

"I suggest we get back to the agenda and then I'll tell you what my first four months have told me."

After some questions and several parallel conversations, Lars again resumed control of the meeting. "Sue is right. I can't say I agree that the required changes will be minor. Frankly, I don't know, because Sue is yet to share with us exactly what her presentation is about. But I agree that we had taken Vendor Managed Inventory to be a shorthand for a customer-centric strategy. Let's get the other agenda items out of the way, and hear what our Ms Hunt has learned."

The appetite for interjection had either been fully met by the earlier exchanges, or was being saved up for Sue later. Whatever the reason, the Board flew through the agreed agenda, attended to personal requirements, replenished coffees, and resumed their seats expectantly.

Sue began. "If our intent is to take a product which has become commoditised, and to win through a superior ability to understand and earn new customers, then the good ship HardBits has four anchors. Anchors are a good thing if your objective is to stay put, but they are not if you are trying to move, as we are." Sue paused long enough to click her PC to have it bring up her first slide.

"I use the anchor as a metaphor. On any given day, any one of these four anchors would be enough to stop us meeting our objectives. If our will is strong and we push hard against this one anchor, we might succeed despite ourselves. But with four anchors down, we don't have a chance."

Sue knew this little piece of theatre was over the top, but her point had been made.

Sales and Marketing are on different planets

Sue's second slide replaced the first. She read the heading, but allowed the Directors to read the bullet points for themselves.

Sales & Marketing are on different planets

Sales sees its job as:
- Presenting our credentials to new prospects
- Building proposals which meet the needs of these prospects
- Gaining their agreement to buy
- Looking after customers so that they want to buy again.

Marketing sees its job as:
- Positioning the HardBits brand through advertising & PR
- Planning and managing campaigns & events
- Producing product collateral to support the sales efforts

After a minute, Justin asked, "So what should it look like Sue?"

"I'll get to what it should look like shortly. Let's look first at why that's a problem." Sue looked down to her notes to make sure she missed none of her points.

"One - our sales people don't get to see enough new prospects. Two - when we bomb out with a prospect, we walk away from them. Who says that just because they didn't buy from us today that they wouldn't do so in three months? Why do we leave them alone?

"And three – our campaigns and events are only getting us awareness, or at best leads. They aren't creating customers."

"But Sue, you never get customers from events." It was Jenny this time.

"I realise that, but a lead should be a half-cooked customer, not a name. If we were to look at leads as prospects that were a part of the way towards becoming a customer, Marketing would only be creating leads for prospects that look like the sort of companies who will probably buy from us.

"That might sound obvious, but right now, Marketing produces leads and hands them to Sales. The problem is that Marketing sees their job as done at that point, because that's all they were asked to do. The leads though, are just names, not opportunities. They are not the sort of companies who we know will become customers. In fact, they are so bad that Sales don't even bother following them up."

Sue continued. "What are the key pieces of the problem? Marketing sees Sales as an internal customer. Sales sees Marketing as a service provider, and each believes they could find a better one outside the company if they were allowed to."

Lars muttered. This was exactly what he was referring to when he made his 'address' about working on the same team. But Sue didn't notice Lars' agreement, and continued.

"The reason we have this problem, and many other companies do too, is that there is no shared framework for them to work on together. Sales thinks about funnels and pipelines and the sales process, and Marketing thinks about brand awareness and positioning. There is no connection between these. We can't simply ask them to be nice to each other. It's more than that. We need to create a single framework which covers both their worlds."

Sue paused to allow them to collect their thoughts, and perhaps so she could do the same. She was delighted that no-one asked a question in the short minute while she was preparing her next angle. Perhaps they were still digesting her key point about the absence of a common framework.

"Sales people are selfish, focused, driven, and long may it be so. Marketers are creative, take criticism poorly, look at a broader view, and consider the whole success, not a single deal. Long may this be so too. I don't propose to merge them organisationally; neither do I want to blend them into some not quite white and not quite black hybrid. We need these differences. We need, though to resolve:

- Who drives the planning?
- What path are they heading down?
- Around what common 'cause' or process are we planning their respective contributions?
- Who owns each piece of the execution?
- How do we measure success consistently?
- What are we trying to achieve with our aggregate Sales and marketing resources?"

"Sue, this sounds like it's still pretty undefined." Jenny was attuned enough not to let the force of Sue's argument substitute for substance.

"It is, absolutely. But if we are to get any sort of efficiencies, we need Sales and Marketing working on a single plan."

"Let me see if I get this Sue," Jenny continued.

"No-one else is doing this, but you need Sales and Marketing to be separate organisationally, and different in their style, but working to a single cause."

"Yes, and the cause is not revenue. That's too far out of sight from their day to day activities. I can't get on the phone to a sales person or a marketer and say 'Do more revenue.' We need some outcome closer in time to their actions, something more basic, more incremental perhaps, and that deals with our total efforts to earn and transact with customers."

Sue moved to the whiteboard and drew a series of bubbles with an arrow through the middle.

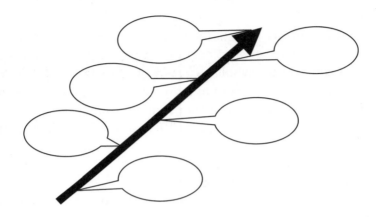

"Here are all the pieces. We need a single **something** that defines an outcome and acknowledges clear steps. As I said, revenue is a final output, but is not useful to make clear the progression, or journey. We need something towards which all the activities of Marketing and Sales are incremental steps. Top right is the end point. Do more of X and you'll inch up. Do more of Y and you'll inch right. We'd expect to see different contributions from each function, and perhaps even from each person, but it needs to be obvious if a given tactic is likely to cause progression or not."

Lars was enjoying Sue's passion, but had not connected at all to her argument. "I can't see where this is leading, but I accept that you are describing the normal interaction, or lack of it, between Sales and Marketing. However, this is an internal issue. Aren't we trying to get closer to the customer?"

"Right, so let's look at the second anchor. To revisit my metaphor though, the disconnection we have been discussing between the activities and focus of Sales and Marketing, which I have identified as one of the anchors, would be enough to prevent us from meeting our objectives even if nothing else was going on. That is even more so for the next anchor." Sue returned to her PC and clicked to bring on her third slide – the second anchor.

Buying process is ignored

Buying process is ignored

I'm ready to sell, I hope you're ready to buy:

- Sales calls on the customer when we want revenue
- If the customer isn't ready to buy, we drop them
- Our ads ask customers to compare us with with competitors
- Our events present product features
- Our Direct Mail letters invite prospects to call us
- We have no idea how our customers buy

Again, Sue read the heading, but not the bullet points. She amplified her theme though by adding "We try to ambush our prospects. We jump out from bushes and say in a loud voice 'I sell plastic, and it's good,' and we assume they are ready to buy from someone and the fact that we sell plastic is of interest to them. Maybe it was last week and isn't this week. Maybe it's not on their radar screen today, but will be in five months."

Jenny leaned forward, "I can see that. But don't all our competitors do the same? I don't want to burst your bubble Sue, but aren't we describing issues which are reasonably well known?"

"Absolutely, that's why this is exciting", Justin interjected. Sue hadn't expected Justin to answer for her, but was thrilled when he did. Even more so when he added: "The issue is that intellectually everyone knows this, but operationally does nothing. Is that your point Sue? If we get this right, we'll be ahead?" Sue nodded.

Jenny continued her enquiry. "So what effect does this ignorance have on the buyer?"

Sue resumed. "For our buyer:
– We show that we have no idea how they buy
– We show that we don't care
– We bother them when they are not ready, and
– Are not around when they want us."

Justin again joined Sue's cause. "Is it any wonder our sales people are not popular?"

"Except with their favourite customers," Jenny offered.

"You are right Jenny. Our customers recognise the importance of getting a sales contact they can work with. He or she is their main conduit into HardBits. That's why I was so cranky when I was at DHM and you gave me four reps in three years. Other customers must have the same issue. But Justin is right also. Prospects don't like our reps, because they are an interruption to them, unless they are in the market to change suppliers.

"Then they are a *necessary* interruption," Justin quipped.

Sue pressed home her advantage, throwing another slide up:

The wrong tactic at the wrong time

"For us, the effect of this disconnect between our timing and the prospect's timing is that our tactics are hopelessly ineffective because we hit them with the wrong tactic at the wrong time."

Jenny was now permanently leaning forward. "You're right Sue. We often discuss why our customers buy, or don't, but I have never been a part of a discussion about how our customers buy. It looks like there are at least three pieces to this: the effect on the customer, the poor return on our investment, and the absence of a framework for changing any of this. So how do you fix this last piece?"

"Frankly I don't know Jenny. I've avoided the temptation to solve this until I was 100% clear that I knew what the problem was.

"What I can say is that our customers and prospects have been conditioned to expect sales people to interrupt them, and marketing tactics like Direct Mail to do the same. They are used to it, and it's a part of their general negativity towards sales people, and to many of the tactics of Marketing.

"We're not going to fix that. If we find some way to change, the rest of the world won't. We might enjoy some success, but our sales people and our marketing tactics will be viewed the same as they are today, perhaps marginally better if we are lucky. They are seeing so many other sales people and marketing tactics that their generally negative view will remain.

"We need to work out what the buying process looks like, then work out where each customer is up to, then help them to get to the end. This way, although they'll initially not be receptive, at least our timing will be right and we stand a better chance of being heard, and perhaps even welcomed."

Lars had been enjoying the friendly banter between Jenny, Justin and Sue. "This sounds to me like the customer is on a journey. Maybe our job is to be their guide." Lars' large hands became his signposts as he animated his otherwise measured contribution. "To help them get from this step to the next. Maybe. Step by step. You are here, let's work together on getting to there."

Graham appeared a little less convinced than his colleagues. "Sounds a bit kind of lefty to me. A bit seventies."

Sue smiled, suspecting Graham was handing her an opportunity to close, but Jenny, not reading the same dynamic, jumped in first. "Sure, we have to mind our language and not presume to be condescending. But I get the notion of thinking about the customer journey. But how do we do this Sue?"

"I think we have to plan our tactics around helping the customer progress. But again, let's not solve it just yet. I want you to stay with me while we lay out the rest of the problem.

Again Sue moved to the whiteboard, being careful not to lose her diagram from the discussion about the disconnect between Sales and Marketing. She drew a road. "As Lars suggested, it's like the customer is on a journey. We have no idea of where they are up to in their journey. So we jump out from behind a rock and say 'you want to buy? Because we sure want to sell when you're ready.' The ones we bag are the ones we were lucky enough to hit at the right time. Pot luck."

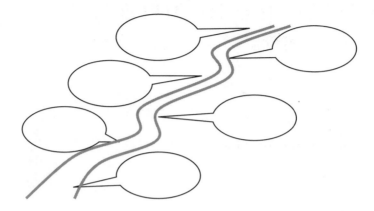

Justin was warming. "OK Sue, I get this one. You are somewhat turning marketing thinking on its head. I don't mind that."

"Marketing *and* Sales Justin," she corrected. "This is about the total process of earning more customers and revenue. It challenges the way this aggregate Sales and Marketing resource is traditionally planned."

But then Sue realised that they were all assuming they had invented something new here, and that was a considerable overstatement. She started forming words in her mind to remind them of the fact that the notion of buyer behaviour was hardly new to either Marketing or to Sales, but that the issue was that their day-to-day activities showed no recognition of this knowledge. They did not *operationalise* this knowledge.

Although important, this realisation didn't help her cause with the Board. She took the soft road instead. It felt too comfortable that they were all agreeing and contributing, and Sue didn't feel like changing that. She let them enjoy their momentary feeling of original intellect.

"OK, let's keep rolling here." Sue glanced at her watch. She was going to have to pedal a little faster if she was to get through all four anchors before lunch. She returned to her PC to move to the next slide.

Tactics are arbitrary

Tactics are arbitrary

We have no idea why we:

- Publish a newsletter
- Advertise
- Attend tradeshows
- Run in-house events
- Send Direct Mail letters
- Email clients and prospects
- Cold call prospects
- Call on customers

"We have no idea why we do what we do. I'm being extremely unkind, of course. Some of these tactics are great, and some less so, but great for what? Let's say we decided tomorrow to enter a new country. What tactics should be included in our mix and what should not? How do we know which tactics will best help us? So we do some 'stuff.' Some of the tactics are logical and successful; others seem sensible but are not. How do we work out before we go which tactics to use?

"Or, let's say someone in the team reads a good book like *Permission Marketing* by Seth Goddin and decides that opt-in email marketing is a winner. This is an email marketing campaign where we only send emails to people who expressly give us their permission to send them that email, but the details are not important.

"So, anyway, let's say someone reads the book and decides it's a winner. Great, but a winner at what? Most of what we do, and what everyone else does, is a solution looking for a problem. Permission marketing might be perfect for us, or it might be completely wrong. How do we decide?

"Look at our customer newsletter. It has a little bit of everything: product news, staff changes, customer testimonials, and industry issues. Exactly what are we trying to achieve, and for exactly which audience?"

"But Sue, aren't you now launching a broadside at *everything* about the marketing science?" Justin asked.

"Again Justin, this is Marketing *and* Sales. What I am saying is that if we commissioned development of some new software for our Manufacturing, the developers would follow a pretty well-worn process to develop then test …"

Sue stopped; the analogy was not a strong one. She hadn't answered Justin's question, she didn't necessarily mean to launch such a broad assault on the marketing science, and her analogy wasn't going to help. She paused to collect her thoughts.

"Sue, may I have a go?" It was Graham.

Graham usually left the boardroom banter to the other Directors. Since he had relinquished his role as CEO three years ago, Graham had allowed himself to become something of a boffin. It seemed strange to hear him interrupt. This must have been the effect for the others also, because the room fell silent.

"These are all connected. If we are saying that Sales and Marketing need to work to a single agenda, and that the agenda should be built around the buying process rather than the selling process, then oughtn't the tactics be selected to cause progression from one stage in the buying process to the next? Isn't the question not 'what should I do with my newsletter?', but 'how can I get the prospects from here to there?'"

Sue stared blankly at Graham. For all her clarity of thought on the weekend, she had not thought to point out that there was such a causal link between each of the anchors.

"Do you disagree?"

"Pardon me, Graham." Sue realised she had been staring. "No, I agree." It was the best she could manage. She was still thinking about the link and why she had not brought this out.

Sue added some arrows to her drawing on the whiteboard.

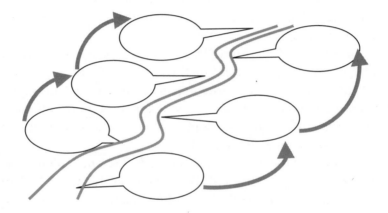

As she drew, Sue asked out aloud, perhaps to herself, or perhaps to the Directors. "So what is the journey? How do we plan for it *in aggregate?* And what does it take to cause a mass migration from stage one to stage two, and so on?"

"Surely we wouldn't get all our customers moving at the same time?"

"No, you're right Justin, there's still some thinking to do. And there is more to the puzzle."

Lars had a sparkle in his eyes. This was going so much better for Sue than the previous Board meeting. "But we are onto something here Sue. What is the fourth leg of this thing? You are teasing us again."

Our indicators tell us nothing

Our indicators tell us nothing

- The sales forecast is way too late
- We measure outputs against plan, but not inputs
- We don't benchmark:
    - Sales against sales internally
    - Sales or Marketing externally
    - Tactics against other tactics

"We sweat the sales forecast, but can't do anything about it.

"Every Monday the Sales Managers get together with Brett and they sweat the forecast. They are micro-managing the hot prospects as you'd expect, but who is fixing next quarter's deficit? And who knows if there is one to fix?

"Let me set this up carefully. The small number of deals we think we're going to win come from the slightly larger number of deals we feel good about, which in turn come from the larger number of deals we have a chance at, etcetera. This is normal opportunity management, and we do it like everyone else does.

"Think of each probability as a bucket, full of prospects. The buckets get smaller, that is fewer members, the higher the probability. The issue is that we only manage the smaller buckets, full of high probability prospects. If the sales forecast is looking sick, it means we are short of members in these later stages. Fine. Again, this is the reality everyone faces.

"We assume, though, that if we run low on high-probability prospects, there will be plenty of lower-probability prospects to fill the gap. But get this: we have absolutely no idea if we have plenty available to fill the gap, or none.

"We need to know now if we have enough prospects at 5%, and 10%, not just the opportunities which we have progressed to have a 50% or better chance of closing. And how many is enough? We need measurement systems that give us enough warning to fix the problem. It would be like only finding out your tank was empty when you were 300 kilometres from the nearest station."

Sue had been talking without pause, and should have been tiring. She was not.

"There's more to it also. I want you to focus your attention on the notion of us relying on a forecast that is measuring only the last stages of the journey. But broaden it a bit also.

"We are not benchmarking any of the sales or marketing initiatives between the sales teams, against the competition, or against companies in other industries. We don't benchmark cold calls, close rates, etcetera for Sales, or readership rates, brand awareness, advertising effectiveness for Marketing.

Sue was pumping now. She wanted to tease this one out fully before they ran out of time, or attention. "The issue is as simple as measurement, but it touches so many aspects of what we do. It also has planning implications. How many prospects do we need to read our Direct Mail, or attend our seminar, etc? How many prospects need to see a sales person? We have no idea."

Sue stopped and looked at the Directors. They had allowed her to lay out her argument fully before interrupting. It took a moment for them to realise that she was done before Jenny broke the silence. "Sue, I buy all this, but how come this dark picture hasn't dawned on others also?"

"Well, it has Jenny. It's just that everyone has always forgiven Sales and Marketing this lack of measurement believing it to be too hard. And is it not?"

"I don't know, we have never tried." Jenny spoke with authority having formerly been HardBits' Sales Director.

"Enough said." Lars punctuated for Sue. "OK Sue, do your whiteboard thing." He waived with his hands towards the whiteboard, as if directing traffic. "I'm keen to agree what we're going to do about this new found enlightenment."

"No need to whiteboard this one Lars. These steps are already enough," Sue pointed to the arrows. "The question is not just 'what are we going to do?' but 'how many?' and 'when?'

"Here's what I propose. I admitted to you when I started that my intent was only to acknowledge the problem, not yet to find a solution. Do you agree that we have those problems at HardBits?"

No one answered. "Seriously, do we have those problems?" Again, Sue waited for an answer.

Jenny and Justin obliged with a perfunctory, "Yes."

Sue realised this was the best she would get from them, so she abandoned the approach. "Good, that's all I wanted for today. I have my team working on some key inputs, although I haven't yet told them why. I will now that I have your agreement. At our next meeting at the beginning of March, I'll have my answers. And whilst I don't yet know what they will be, I doubt the changes are going to require Board approval.

"This can change without adding to our resources. Thank you - not just for hearing me out, but also for shaping this discussion. I have enjoyed your contributions."

Sue ate lunch alone. Jenny and Justin had invited her to debrief with them over lunch, but she was pretty exhausted and needed to let it all settle in. Her next audience was her management team. Graham was already on board, but she'd have to win Kyle, Brett and Warren (and Sarah for that matter) without his help.

Will it make the boat go faster?

The strong espresso after lunch had hit the spot, and Sue was cycling her thoughts quickly. Sue knew that everything boiled down to these four problems:
– Sales and Marketing are on different planets;
– The buying process is ignored;
– Tactics are arbitrary;
– Our indicators tell us nothing.

There were other issues that hinged around these, but if she changed the business to address these problems, then she had it. No matter how she looked at the problems though, they gave no insight into what should be done. There was no obvious link between problem and solution.

Sue pondered the idea of telling her staff that she could see the problem, and not the solution. Thinking with her pen, she wrote on the back of her business card.

> The challenge is not to address the problems head-on, but to build an approach to customer acquisition for which these problems do not exist.

This wasn't quite it. She scratched 'an approach' and replaced it with 'a business.' Better, but still too long.

Why do I need to fix the problems? What will be different if we do? More revenue? More customers? More business? She was running out of business cards as she pondered, scribbled, read, discarded, pondered.

Earn more customers

It would do for now. *So, how can we earn more customers in a way that didn't...* she stopped. Sue realised she was following the SPIN process Brett had introduced her to. Situation, Problem, Implication, and Need/Payoff. The *problem* was the four anchors; and the *need* was a way of accelerating and improving the acquisition of new customers. Sue's resolve that her management team be briefed quickly changed; she needed them to help form the answer, not just do the homework.

They might already have the answer without realising it.

Helen managed to get Sue's management team together for two hours the following day without too much difficulty. Sue remained standing after her colleagues had taken a seat at the table.

"OK, you've all provided inputs that have led me to a realisation. Maybe you already saw what am I about to show you, but for me it was a revelation. I picked your brains, and then I asked each of you to do some homework over the last month.

"I was planning to pull this together myself, but realised yesterday that we need to form the answer together. For that reason, I want to tell you what I think the problem is. But here's the thing, and listen up guys because the detail is key.

"I'm going to tell you the problem. Actually it's four problems, but I'm not going to table them until each of you is 100% clear on what February is all about. It is this: I don't want you to try to fix the problem, at all. And I'm not going to either.

"Do the homework I have asked you to drive. But as you do the homework, and go about your business generally, let your mind range around the problems. Again, don't try to solve them. Think of the problems as things we want to go away, rather than things we want to be driven by. If we focus on fixing them, we'll be limited. We have to focus on other things, and in the process, to fix them. Stick with me here. I know this sounds a little unclear, but I'm hoping to make it clear.

"Now, let me shift to what we *do* need to do at the end of February - create a new approach to earning new business." She paused for effect. And then to underscore her point, "We need to learn to earn new business better than we do today.

"There is nothing new about that, but every approach to earning customers I have ever seen in action, or read about, either makes one or more of these four problems worse, or in the least it reinforces them.

"So, we need to learn how to earn more customers, and whatever approach we adopt needs not only to address this need, but also address the four problems."

"Sue, maybe I can help." Sue felt she was doing just fine and didn't need Brett's help, but paused to let him continue anyway. "What you are saying is sounding awfully like SPIN, which we use for planning and managing sales calls. The need is what customers want, and the problem is why. Same here right? The need is to get more customers, and the problem is what you're about to show us."

Sue chuckled. "Brett, I saw the link with SPIN also, in fact it helped me to understand what I was looking at and why I needed the team's help. But I should have known you'd have a clearer perspective. I only read the book once. You call it your bible."

Kyle wasn't going to be outdone. "I don't know about SPIN Sue, but I get what you're asking us to do. Address the need, which is earn new customers, and in the end we'll see whether we have made the problem worse, or better."

"Close enough Kyle. So here goes. I call them the four anchors, and here's why."

The presentation was well received. Sue had considered watering it down in the fear that her managers would think she was having a swipe at them, but she had been careful enough in her preparatory comments to avoid this.

"So, reactions? To what extent does that describe our situation?"

"*Problems* Sue. If you are going to use the SPIN model, the *situation* is what is going on, the *problem* is the pain this situation creates."

"OK Brett, I've got it."

"Sorry, Sue I wasn't being a smart Alec." Everyone laughed at Brett's attempt to position himself somewhat differently from the picture they universally held of him. He got it, and rephrased. "OK, maybe I *was* being a smart Alec. What I meant is that I wasn't *trying* to be a smart Alec. My point was this: whether or not we buy into the problems is surely not key. What is key is that we buy into the need, right?" The nods were meant to convey "Go on," but they were less than Brett wanted.

Realising nods were all he going to get at this stage, Brett continued. "So, here's my deal. If we are looking for a way to earn more customers, why aren't we looking at *existing* methodologies. Surely someone else has this need too?"

"That's just it Brett. Everyone has the need, well almost everyone. But do they have the same problems? I don't think so. Think of the methodologies you use, or have used, had pitched to you or you've read about. Do any of them *fully* avoid the four anchors?"

Brett was quiet for a full minute. Sue prepared to offer another comment, but Brett held up his hand as if to say "Just a minute." Then he looked up at Sue and asked simply, "When do we start?"

The others said nothing, just looked straight at Sue waiting for her answer. Sue knew that she had a team.

From: Sue Hunt

Sent: Tuesday 5 February

To: Graham Chase
                 Brett Marsden
                 Kyle Hoffman
                 Warren Jackson

Subject: Earning more customers

Team

Thanks for your support today. This is a journey for all of us, and I appreciate your decision to give me your full support.

We have the four anchors, they are:

—   Sales and Marketing are on different planets;
—   The buying process is ignored;
—   Tactics are arbitrary;
—   Our indicators tell us nothing.

What we need is to learn to earn more customers (faster). We'll need a new approach, not just some new skills.

We have some homework for the balance of the month which I've discussed with you previously. No changes to these instructions.

Now, just one more thing as you are going about your work. Look for clues. What ideas, inputs or constraints are going to shape our new approach? Don't try to build it, just look for clues.

We'll meet Monday 4 March from 8 till 10 for the first of a series of management team workshops that will continue every Monday until we have 'cracked the nut.' Usual operational meetings remain the same. Our Monday workshops will be held in the meeting room off my office. Until further notice, this room is our war room, and is unavailable for other meetings. We'll deal with one input idea each week, and we'll keep going until we have the answers. I don't care if we take six months. We'll keep on until we've nailed it.

Any questions or issues, come see me.

Best, Sue

Sue's phone rang shortly afterwards. "Sue, hi, it's Kyle. I've just read your note about the war room. Looks fine and I'm looking forward to it. OK, would you be happy for Sarah to participate in those meetings? She's great on process and can do lots of the be-tween-meeting work."

"Great idea Kyle. Agreed." It was good to see Kyle unthreat-ened by Sarah's contribution.

Sue reflected: *Now that we know the question, from where will the answer come?*

Mosaic

Chipping away

The pressures of the normal operations of the business quickly took Sue's mind from the task she had just consigned for herself and her management team. She had been neglecting a few matters over the last week, and her attention was quickly absorbed for the rest of February. She shot out a weekly reminder to the team to keep their eyes open for clues, but was not giving it much thought herself.

February raced past, and even provided opportunity for Sue to regain a little balance to her world.

"So, let's try some chipping shall we?" Sue's golf pro suggested.

Sue followed Robin to the edge of the practice green. He had selected a 7-iron, 9-iron, pitching wedge and sand wedge. The bucket of balls was still half full after their short session on the mats.

"Grab the wedge, and chip half a dozen into the hole for me."

Sue looked at him smiling. "I wish."

Robin indicated a chipping motion with his arms. "Go on then."

Sue did a workman like job of chipping, and even got one to sink from the edge of the green. Robin collected the balls by deftly flicking each with the 7-iron into his bucket. Even the one in the hole. "So how did that feel? OK? Were you happy with that?"

"OK, I suppose."

"When you hit a nice one, what are you thinking?"

"About holing it mainly."

"No, I mean, what is going on in your mind?"

"Holing it."

"Not the outcome Sue, what are you thinking about?"

"I don't get you Robin. I visualise a nice chip, plopping right onto the landing spot I've picked, then rolling into the hole."

"Good, and when you set up, what are you thinking?"

"The same, I see the hole, and I see my ball going in."

"Ah, got it. Sue, you're thinking about the output, and you need to think about the input. You need a framework for your chipping. You need to know if you're looking to scoop up, hit down, and drive through. You see?"

"But aren't they the minor mechanical movements?"

"No, absolutely no. You need a framework for a chip, for a putt, for a pitch, a drive. Each stroke has a framework, and then you work out the mechanical movements. Your chip, for example, is a punch. Your frame is a punch. The ball will loft itself, that's not your job, that's why the engineers make you a beautifully lofted wedge." Robin's hands became wedges of varying loft to illustrate his points.

"You set up to punch it into the ground, and the wedge will plop you onto the green. You punch, it plops. If you are thinking about the plop and the trickle, then you'll try to scoop the ball. Which, by the way, is what you are doing. Now let me show you."

Nothing Robin did or said was going to make Sue a scratch golfer, but she had learned from past experience with him that after a few weeks of practice she would have the basics right and Robin would let her move onto something else.

At a handicap of 16 Sue was not unhappy with her golf, but since starting her lessons with Robin her average had blown out to 22. Her target was 12. Lessons were a necessary evil, her golf buddies and she had agreed, but it didn't help Sue's confidence that one of her group had not shot a round of over 80 since she was 18.

Sue was no fanatic, but an old pitching wedge that her predecessor had left in the cupboard after he left had found its way into Sue's hands once or twice when she found the need for a break between meetings.

Robin's words from the previous week came back. "If you are thinking about the plop and the trickle, then you'll try to scoop the ball."

Hit down. She glanced at the whiteboard in her office as if it were a green. *Forget about the hole, think about the punch.*

Sue looked at the whiteboard again. Maybe that's it. Sue moved quickly into the war room. Well, she'd broken her own promise and used the room for other meetings since, but she had come to think of it as the war room because she knew it would fill that role for a while.

On the empty whiteboard, she penned the words that would come to form many of their thoughts in the months ahead.

"The inputs shape the outputs."

Sue grabbed the research report Kyle had commissioned. He had chosen not to use the ad agency for a pure research job, and Sue suspected this might have been a good call. (If the answer is advertising, what is the question?)

The report was excellent. Well written, appeared to be thorough, and began with a great three-page executive summary dealing with the three objectives for the research: what the market wants and how they perceive the suppliers; who they are buying from; and how they buy.

Sue turned to the first page of the summary. The message supported Kyle's premise.

What customers said they wanted was reliability of supply. No one was positioned strongly on that, and HardBits in particular was known for high quality and innovation. Nice things to be but not what the market said it wanted. The recommendation was to reposition on reliability of supply and make some changes to ensure they could live up to the revised promise.

The second page had little to say about who the respondents were buying from that wasn't already known to her from the industry analysts' reports.

Sue got to the third page quickly. How they buy. Nothing offered gave her any great inspiration, but she decided that the buying process would be their first war room subject. She could com-
bine these findings and Sarah's work on buying processes generally.

So, where was she?

—   *The inputs shape the output. ('If you are thinking about the plop and
     the trickle, then you'll try to scoop the ball.')*
—   *Need to reposition the brand around reliability of supply and make
     some changes to support this new position.*
—   *Buying process seems pretty consistent from one company to the
     next.*

No magic links here, but maybe the answer would come in pieces.
Perhaps Sue had to build the picture from a collection of pieces. *Let
the mosaic begin.*

A customer journey

"Welcome to the war room," Sue said rather grandly.

"You'll remember from the beginning of the month that although we identified four anchors, our focus is on learning how to earn more customers. As we go, we'll test to ensure we have not reintroduced the problems, but we'll focus on our need.

"Our first challenge is going to be creating a framework. A way of thinking."

Sue spared them the story of the golf lesson, believing it to be a little trivial, and chose to focus just on what she now believed to be key. It was still written on the whiteboard.

"The inputs shape the outputs." Sue read it out loud for reinforcement.

"Our challenge is to create a framework which will shape the inputs. Let's start though with buying process. I asked Sarah to look at the marketing literature to see what the academics are offering in terms of the buying process.

"Sarah, as I understand it, you drew a blank."

"No Sue, worse than a blank. I got heaps and had to sift through it. Unfortunately, it all hinged around retail buyers rather than business buyers. It's the same problem I always encounter: so little of the marketing literature is about business buyers and markets.

"What little I did find that talked of business buyers was very situational – hard to glean any generic findings from that."

"OK, thanks Sarah. Kyle has something though. The market research you did through Feb dealt with three issues. One of them was how they buy. Perhaps you could share that?"

"Sure Sue. Are we going to cover the other outcomes from the research though, because I found the branding findings very useful? Probably more so than the buying process to be frank."

"I'm with you Kyle, we've discussed them off line and I agree the others would enjoy reading them. For now though, I'd like to focus on the buying process."

Kyle began. "It seems most of the buyers have a pretty standard process they follow. They use different language, and there are some subtle variations, but it's pretty much the same with them all." He drew on the board as he spoke.

- Define the need
- Business case
- Select vendors
- Seek proposals
- Select vendor
- Engage

"That's it," said Brett. "That's pretty much what they *think* they do."

"How do you mean 'think they do'?" asked Kyle defensively.

"Well, they say they don't select vendors until they have a business case approved, but that's rubbish. The business case is formed around someone's view of the solution. By the time the business case goes up, they already have their vendors in mind, if not selected.

"Also, they talk to us all the time before they have the need clear. How do you think they get to know what is possible? These guys don't operate in a vacuum. It's something of a journey. They chat to a few people, they find out what others are doing, they prioritise their needs, they get a sense of the costs and the payoff. It's more complex than that." Brett sat down again.

"Any other disagreements?" Sue asked.

"Yeah, when we lose, we lose for a bunch of different reasons. They take us down a certain way and we think we have it, then we lose. I think the 'select vendor' has more steps than that." Brett was still sitting, but was clearly not done.

Kyle was a little less defensive when he asked Brett, "Long before they are clear about what they need, they have the vendors positioned?"

"Sure, it's a shoe box thing. They put us in shoe boxes early. If you're not in the shoe box, like is often the case for us, you don't get to play."

"But is it consistent? Can you say that they all go through the same process?"

"No, not the same *process*, I don't believe so. But they all have to jump through the same hoops, eventually, and they probably go through them in the same order, just that their means of jumping through the hoops differs."

"Can you tell which ones they've jumped through?"

"Sure."

Graham chimed in. "I see it like this Sue. Like we agreed last time, there is a customer journey. Think of it like a train journey. There are stops along the way. People take different paths to each stop, but they have to get through one, or at least they tend to get through it, before they move to the next." Graham was arranging glasses on the table to symbolise the stages of the journey.

"It's a customer journey, and there are states, or stages, they move through. As they get off the train they mutter something like: 'I know what I need and I know what the payoff is.' Then when they get off at the next station they say 'I know what my options are'."

Brett interjected. "And there's some illogical stuff beforehand. The theory says they don't talk to vendors until they have a need, but they do, as I've said. Oh yeah, and they short list also. First they choose two or more potential suppliers, then they choose the one."

Sue pulled an easel away from the wall. She had a fresh pack of butcher's paper suspended on the frame, and drew the stages they had discussed on a timeline before asking, "How's that?"

"OK" replied Brett. "But there's one more. Before they have a need, they have pain. Until something is hurting them, they don't have a need. In fact, there are two more: acknowledge pain, and before they acknowledge it, they're fat, dumb and happy." This met with chuckles. "They don't even know they've got a problem."

"That's a bit condescending Brett, don't you think?"

"Relax, mate. I'm fat, so I can say it OK? It's just an expression."

"No, you dill. I meant it was condescending to suggest that we know they have pain and they don't."

"No I'm serious Kyle. If you've got pain, you probably know it. But before you know it, you are complacent. There is a step before pain, called 'no pain', or maybe 'I don't know I've got pain', or 'I don't acknowledge I have pain.'" Brett was rambling a little.

Sue made a couple of changes. The result looked like meat on a skewer. "It's rough, but it'll do for now."

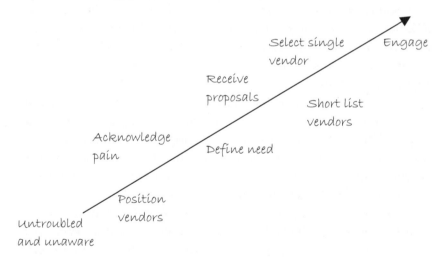

Sarah studied the flow, and said "I'm still uncomfortable with *Position vendors* being early in the process."

"It's real Sarah," said Brett. "Remember what I said earlier. They'll never acknowledge it, but a lot happens before they know they have a need, and sometimes the vendors actually create the need. Believe me, we've got the order right."

"So what's next?" asked Warren, who hadn't spoken until now.

Sarah stood up, remembering that she had a facilitator's role. "That's it for now guys, we need to keep to our time limit. This is going to be a long race."

"Hang on Sarah." Sue moved to the whiteboard. She pointed to her note, as she had earlier, and read out aloud: "The inputs shape the outputs. If we're saying the customer is on a journey, shouldn't our job be to lead them?"

"Maybe," said Brett non-committedly. "Maybe we're their guide, maybe we're not. But whatever we do should be done in order to ensure they get to their next stage."

"Isn't that the same thing? I mean, aren't we leading them?"

"Some. Some customers will let us be their guide, and that's OK. Some won't though. They'll resist even. But whatever we do, we have to make sure that if they're untroubled today, then they better acknowledge pain some time soon otherwise we can't do anything for them."

"That's it guys!" Sue had stayed near her note on the whiteboard, and was now pounding the board with the palm of her hand. "This is the framework for the inputs - customer progression. Our tactics, even our strategies, must be about causing progression, one step at a time. We choose our tactics and strategies based on how well they contribute to the journey."

"Or the other way around, perhaps Sue." Graham seemed to be intent on saving himself for the moments of truth. "What progression do we need, and what tactic will cause that progression?"

They had the beginning of their framework.

"Sarah, can you be scribe?" asked Sue. "Even an MBA can take notes. OK?" Sarah nodded, it was a cheap shot, but she wasn't going to get precious. She was enjoying the energy of discovery.

Sue hadn't done a good job of allowing Sarah to be the facilitator, and was not in the mood to relinquish just yet. "We're not done yet and it's almost 10 already. Does anyone have anything they can't put off if we continue for another hour?" No answer. "Fine, I want to recap on this discussion about the customer journey, and look at measurement systems. We'll see if there is a link."

The funnel leaks

Warren had brought coffees for everyone. He was a hero.

"OK, let's get started." Sue was pumped. "We had a bit of fun earlier. Our own journey led to the discovery of the customer journey. What we need to look at is measurement and benchmarking, and I think they're very related. If we could measure how many start the journey and how many end it, we'd know how many we need to start with."

"This sounds like classic sales funnel stuff to me Sue," volunteered Brett.

"What?" Warren wasn't very tolerant with jargon. "I get the pipeline, but the funnel?"

"Sorry, they're both kind of the same thing. The pipeline is what we put into the forecast, and the funnel is that, plus the stuff we wouldn't dare put on the list because it's way too early."

"So why the funnel?"

"It's a metaphor - lots at the top and a few at the bottom, Brett answered. "It's a visual thing. Anyway, the notion of the funnel isn't mine, it's been used by sales forces for eons. Start with many, end with few. You want to measure that Sue, no probs."

"OK, so let's look at what we've got for measurement, Warren."

"Sue asked me to speak to a dozen CFOs in other organisations to look at what means they use to measure their sales and marketing effectiveness. Here's what's commonly used." Like Kyle had earlier, Warren wrote as he spoke.
- Market share
- Brand awareness
- Marketing spend per revenue $

- Opportunity coverage
- Close rates
- Cold calls per meeting
- Sales activity.

"One I spoke to also measures 'non-compete' rate. That is, how many deals they don't hear about until after they've closed."

Sarah was writing furiously. "Can you explain what you mean by each of the other terms? Actually, just the last four. I can guess what might be meant by them, but what do *you* mean?"

Warren's reply was a little technical. "'Opportunity coverage' is a measure of the multiple of the budget revenue that can be seen in the forecast. The required rate of coverage that can be seen in the forecast is usually something like 2-times or 3-times the budget to allow for unexpected failure or delay.

"'Close rates' is simple - what percentage of proposals submitted do they win? 'Cold calls' counts how many telephone calls a rep has to make to get one meeting. And 'sales activity' varies. Typically it's proposals offered, or meetings held, and it comes down to managing individual reps, whereas mostly the others are for the organisation as a whole."

Sue was confused. "So what do we do with that information Warren? We use most of these measures too."

"We do, a little, but we do it sporadically. Only one of the companies I spoke to is really into this stuff. They're the one that also measured non-compete rates."

Sue persisted. "If we threw that list out, and went back to what we discussed last week. What would we measure?"

"Do you mean would we measure the customer journey?"

"I don't know, what do you think? How does this sound? Measure each stage of the journey. How many make it from stage one to stage two? And how many of them make it to stage three, etcetera?"

"Sounds like Brett's funnel again."

"Sure, but very granular, and built around the customer journey rather than the sales process. Measure our success rate for each stage, and maybe track it over time."

Warren became mischievous. "Time too. Can we track how long it takes? When half the reps promise revenue in June I know we won't see it until September, or later."

Brett got where Warren was going. "You're not having a go at BJ by any chance Warren?" Brett and Warren exchange glances and enjoyed the joke. BJ was well known for his optimistic estimates of how long it would take a customer to make a decision to buy.

"Sure, he's notorious."

Sue joined the giggle for a brief moment, then, "Back to the game guys. So we have a journey, and we know how long it takes, on average to get from A to B, and we know how many people get off at each point. We can track our success and measure if we are getting better.

"How about planning? We could use the benchmarks to work out how many we need to start with to get our revenue." Warren was excited at the prospect of greater revenue predictability.

The mood was electric, and it was more than the effect of Warren's coffee, although that probably had a lot to do with it.

Kyle had been quiet for a while before looking up with a smile. "Hey Brett, you know your funnel?"

"Yup."

"It leaks."

"Say what?"

"It leaks. It's got holes in it. With a normal funnel, everything that goes in the top comes out the bottom. With your funnel, you put 100 in the top and only 10 get out at the bottom."

Kyle was trying too hard to be clever. "OK smarty, it's just a metaphor."

"No, I'm serious Brett. What we're talking about is a leaky funnel, and measuring leakage at each point."

"Sounds like a sieve more likely." Warren was keeping up with them.

"Yeah, maybe," countered Kyle, "But a leaky funnel is actually a better metaphor because you can picture a top to bottom process, with clear stages, and leakage at each stage."

"11 o'clock guys." Sue still hadn't handed over facilitation to Sarah properly. Sue got up again and pulled out the easel. "Let's see what we're saying. We've got a funnel, a leaky funnel, and each level describes a stage in the customer journey. Maybe we should redraw last week's model Sarah. Do you want to have a crack at a graphic to pick up on what we're discussing?"

"How can you draw a funnel inside a 2x2 matrix Sarah?" asked Warren playfully, referring to the stereotype of MBA graduates who seem to distil everything into a four-box matrix from one textbook or another. Sarah glared, then smiled, and hoped someone else would cop Warren's friendly jibe next time.

From: Sarah Martin

Sent: Monday, 11 March

To: Sue Hunt
              Graham Chase
              Brett Marsden
              Kyle Hoffman
              Warren Jackson

Subject: The leaky funnel

How does this look?

Regards, Sarah

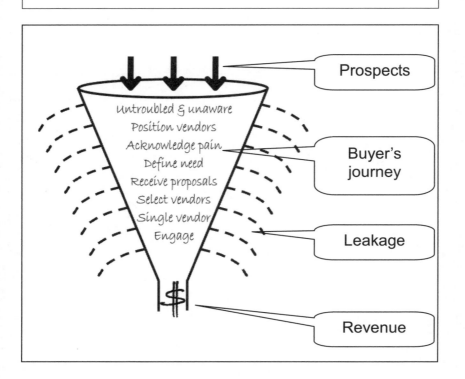

From:	Sue Hunt
Sent:	Tuesday, 12 March
To:	Sarah Martin
CC:	Graham Chase
	Brett Marsden
	Kyle Hoffman
	Warren Jackson
Subject:	Re: The leaky funnel

Well done, Sarah. I like the graphic.

Guys, I feel we made good progress yesterday. I found it useful to look at what other companies are measuring. Even though we didn't adopt these for now, I'd like to keep this subject open. Let's see where the leaky funnel takes us and review Warren's list again soon.

Best, Sue

Sue knew they had started well. They ran the risk, of course, of believing their rhetoric, but the team was beginning to work well together, and Sue genuinely felt they were onto something. As she looked at Sarah's diagram of the leaky funnel, she thought about when she had been a customer of HardBits. Was this how she bought? Was she typical? What would make one group of buyers progress quickly, and another slowly, or not at all? How should they look at buyers? As a single group, or as multiple groups?

They had an awfully long way to go.

As thick as thieves

Brett lined up with a few of his better reps and joined them on sales calls during the week. He normally liked to join at least two customer meetings a week, and expected his Sales Managers to go on no fewer than four per week. This week though, he had a unique purpose.

The meeting with Kitchen King had been defining. Kitchen King was a major competitor to Tupperware, but sold through traditional retail outlets. Their success came largely from the convenience of the channel rather than the quality of their product. For all that, Kitchen King recognised that their supplier of plastic could help them to meet tight supply deadlines triggered by demand that had proven to be hard to predict. Their relationship with their supplier of plastic beads was therefore a close, strategic alliance. Unfortunately, that relationship was not with HardBits.

Brett's call was to debrief after having lost the tender to the incumbent – Sartle. Garry Winsome, the Manufacturing Director, was frank in his debrief. Once Brett felt they had extracted all they could from the debrief, he changed tack.

"Garry, we accept your decision and thank you for your candour in helping us understand why we were not successful on this occasion. But I want to ask you something unrelated to HardBits and our bid. Can you spare another five minutes?"

"Sure."

"Thanks. If you could change all the bead manufacturers that bid for this work at once, what change would you make?"

"Easy. I'd have them all hold greater stocks of each of the grades of plastic we use, and have them operate large fleets of trucks so they could deliver on demand." Garry was only half kidding, but he knew he was asking for the impossible.

Brett expected this, and was ready. Simply, "why?"

"Because we need flexible supply."

"Why?"

"Because we don't want too much or too little."

"Why?"

The rally continued for a long time, and surprisingly, Garry didn't tire of it, realising that Brett's digging could do no harm as the contract had already been relet to Sartle.

The basis of Garry's answers was Kitchen King's inability to manage demand from their retailers. They suspected that the retailers were not managing their ordering efficiently, but were in no mood to take them on over this, preferring to accommodate the variable demand – even making a virtue of their ability to meet this variability.

Back at the War Room on Monday morning, Warren had again supplied the coffees. As with the previous week, this proved to be a very popular move. He sensed he was not contributing much to the debate other than to lift the energy level of the first hour courtesy of his caffeine hit.

"Fellow travellers," Sue began. "We had a great session last week. We turned the buying process upside down and worked out that the funnel leaks. Seriously though, this was good. What I want to focus on today is whether everyone cycles at the same rate. Do some prospects go faster than others, and will we likely enjoy different rates of success?"

Sarah mused out aloud. "Customers defined by their rates of leakage? I studied many different segmentation methods at uni, but never leakage-based segmentation." It hardly brought the house down, but Sarah enjoyed the collegiate chuckle this evoked.

"So Sarah, what are the more common ways to segment the market?" Sue knew this to be a long suit for Sarah.

"Well, segmenting by industry is popular, but less so than it used to be. Normal demographics like size, industry, and geography are popular, but not very helpful." Sarah moved to the whiteboard. "The main ways to divide up the available market before choosing which pieces to focus on are:
- How they buy
- What they buy
- What they need
- What they believe
- Their size, or
- Their industry."

As others had done, Sarah wrote as she spoke. Partly to fill the aural void, and partly to emphasise her points. "Most of the current thinking though, assumes companies will segment around needs. The products, programs, and channels all need to vary around the differences between needs."

"Thanks Sarah." Sue switched the play. "OK Brett, we asked your guys to look at problems rather than needs. Maybe that was a mistake. Let's see what we've got anyway."

"Well, it was interesting. We have every customer facing one of five problems:
- None
- Uneven demand
- Declining margins
- Lack of capacity
- Excessive holding costs"

"Wow, that's a great list Brett," Warren volunteered. "How solid is it?"

"Rock. I went on calls with reps all last week to validate this, and our customers all pretty much have one of these problems going on. Some have two."

"What can we assume they need as a consequence?"

"There's a range of answers Warren. We use this SPIN methodology on calls, and we find that two customers with the same problem, may have different needs. That is, they want to solve the problem differently."

Sue looked for a link. "So what is the best way to group them Sarah?"

"Well, if we group them by needs, we'll get our product strategy right, because their common needs are largely met by common solutions. That's the most compelling reason for segmenting around needs. If we group them by problem however, we get efficiency from the sales process because we get our messages right, and we look like heroes to the prospects if we understand the problem and work with them on defining it to a need."

"So, Graham." He had been following the conversation fully, but had not felt the need to contribute. Sue wanted him engaged. "If you knew you had a group of buyers all of whom needed the same thing, what would we change about the products?"

"Well not much Sue to be honest. The product is largely homogeneous, it's the way the customer uses it that makes it different."

"Sounds like problems is a better way to group the prospects then, don't you all think?"

Warren turned to Sarah. "Do you think your professors could cope with adding another segmentation strategy? Problem-based segments?"

She chuckled. "I think they'd cope. But I might write the book and be rich and famous first. Frankly, I like this idea. I can see immediately how we would deal with this in Marketing."

"Sales is the same Sarah. We can work with this." Brett, always the salesman, was seeking closure.

But Sarah, the academic, wasn't happy that they had it yet. "Hang on. It's true that if we put prospects into groups based on the similarities in their problems, they might respond similarly to a given message or tactic. But it's also true that they might respond differently.

"For example, if the problem is uneven demand, the attitude to this problem might be different. One prospect might know they have uneven demand, and another might not. The prospect who knows, might be a quick buyer, whilst the other might not realise they have this problem, and it might take a while to work them through this process of acknowledging the problem, defining the need, etcetera.

Sue rejoined the debate. "So, what is it that defines one group differently from another, in a way that we can get some value from? I mean, surely the purpose of putting prospects into groups is to do or offer or price something materially different to each separate group. Otherwise, why have more than one group?"

She looked at Sarah. "Before you write that book, I think there is more work. You need to work out whether we are segmenting on needs, problems, speed, behaviour, or whatever." And then to the larger group, "Back to the funnel then guys.

"Would one group get through at a different rate if they had problem A rather than problem B?"

Brett had been thinking this through. "Maybe, maybe not. Maybe it doesn't matter though. Other things than the leakage can change and have a material difference. So maybe we've not answered your question, but maybe we don't need to.

"The fast versus slow question could happen within a group of prospects defined by what problem they are facing anyway, could it not? That is, maybe we need to acknowledge this as an issue, not as a means of looking at our customers and prospects."

"Agreed." Sue turned to the easel, took a fresh sheet of butcher's paper and drew multiple funnels.

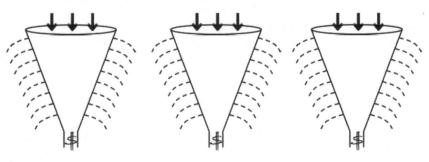

Problem A   Problem B   Problem C

"We set out to explore whether there were rates of different progress, and maybe there are, but maybe that's not key. What appears to be key is that customers can be grouped according to what problem they most face, and we can do something useful with those groups. Sounds like a good point to conclude on. See you next week."

As they got up from their seats, Brett called out, "Hey Warren. I'll get the coffees next week."

"Deal."

"Just before you go guys," Sue raised her voice over the sounds of chairs and papers. "Next week we need to look at how to take a single view of working the funnel - one without barriers between Sales and Marketing. Think about it and bring your ideas to the workshop. See you then. Have a great week."

There's money in recycling

Sue kicked off their third workshop without any fanfare. "We've crafted a customer journey, a leaky funnel, and multiple funnels dealing with separate problems. Each week's progression has been good. Let's take stock. Are we improving our ability to earn more customers?"

"Absolutely," said Brett. His first coffee had been a short espresso thrown down whilst he was waiting for the others' coffees to be made. He was already firing.

Warren disagreed. "I think we are heading in the right direction, but can't yet see that we have changed anything other than the way we think. I need more flesh on the bones before I'd be so bold as to say we have accelerated anything."

"OK," said Sue, regaining control of the conversation. "If we did nothing other than build our tactics around the customer's buying processes, would we be seeing more or less of the four anchors? Let's look at each:
- Sales and Marketing are on different planets
- The buying process is ignored
- Tactics are arbitrary
- Our indicators tell us nothing.

"The only one we've really challenged is the buying process, right?" They all nodded. "So, not wanting to start the day on a down note, but we have a way to go yet, right? OK. Today I want to focus our discussion around the first anchor – the way Sales and Marketing interact.

"Now remember, I said at the outset that the way I want to do this is not to tackle each problem head on, but to build a new approach, a new competency, and then to ensure this new approach addresses each of these four anchors. Having said that, today I want us to think about our approach to earning customers and how Sales and Marketing work on that together."

Sue knew that she had been imprecise in describing how she wanted the team to tackle each issue. On the one hand she was asking them not to think about it and on the other she was. Her own mind was unclear. Somewhere in there were the elements of what she wanted, but they were far from ordered.

"Can I start?" Kyle was already standing making clear he intended to start anyway.

"I'm not so sure we want Sales and Marketing too close. There aren't many of the sales people I'd consider close friends. No offence Brett. They're wired differently. Most of the marketers reckon they could do the sales job better, but none of them could. It takes a special kind of human to sell, day in day out, take rejection and keep going, etcetera. Do we want to change that?"

"I don't know that we do Kyle." Sue was enjoying this. "I'm not saying make them the same, I'm saying that today they are working to different, and disconnected agendas. I want you both on the same agenda, even if you are working on different pieces.

"As part of the digging around Warren talked about last week, I asked him to find out how this was working elsewhere. Before we go there, does anyone else have any observations?"

Brett kept quiet. Sue knew his position on Marketing and this was not the forum to bring it up again.

"OK, Warren..."

"Well, I thought it was only us, but it turns out it is part of the job description for Sales and Marketing to hate each other." Smiles and the odd chuckle. "That's obviously a bit strong, but if I put it more positively, there is a positive friction between the two camps in most companies I spoke to.

"Plastix's sales people admire their marketers, because most of the marketers are technical product guys and girls. They are the gurus. We've kept the technical knowledge in Manufacturing and

Ops, and lend them out as needed, so they are seen as the gurus, not Marketing.

"But I also spoke to my counterpart at Telecom who I went to Uni with. They did something a little closer to what we might be thinking about. You know how, simplistically, Marketing does branding and lead generation, and Sales takes it from there? Well, at Telecom they hand the prospects backwards and forwards depending on where the prospect is up to at the time. They have these programs called incubator programs, where Marketing sort of takes them back to cook them a little more before handing them back again to Sales when they are ready. If Sales fail to get them to buy they hand them back to Marketing and so on. They seem to have it pretty well ironed out so the prospects don't mind, because they don't want to deal with a sales person until they are ready anyway. So it suits them just fine."

Brett smiled. This is what he had complained to Sue about. Marketing gives him dud leads and should take them back if they're no good. He knew he should keep his thoughts to himself, but couldn't help a little 'contribution.' "So, it's sort of a quality assurance policy on leads?"

Kyle shot him a glance, but Sue was onto it. "I don't think that's what Warren said though Brett. As customers progress on their journey, at various times and for various reasons, they fall off the process."

"They leak," Sarah reminded him.

"OK, they leak out of the funnel. Isn't incubation about picking up all the leaked prospects and warming them before putting them back into the funnel?"

Warren wasn't one for allowing people, even his boss, to put words into his mouth. "Well I'm pretty sure that's not what Telecom are saying either Sue, but it's probably how we would want to look at it. I'm reasonably comfortable they are not discussing the leaky funnel and strategies to recycle their leakage. It's probably the same thing though."

"Or maybe not, Warren." Sue sensed something useful was going to emerge from this discussion. "Brett, if you had 100 new prospects we had never dealt with before, how many could become customers?"

"Maybe 25% of them."

"But in one go, how many could you convert?"

"Maybe one in twenty, so five out of the hundred."

"Then you'd cook them a little longer and have another go at the failures at another time and that's how you get to the 25?"

"Something like that. That's how it works today."

"No it's not Brett, and that's just my point." Sue definitely had the scent. "All our planning, Sales and Marketing, has been around success. Do this to them, then do this to them, etcetera. Although we don't talk about it, we know that we lose a few with each iteration.

"Let's rebuild that around our customer journey. We start with 100 who are untroubled and unaware. Maybe 80 leak out because they don't have the pain or the need, at least at this stage, and 20 go on to seek proposals and we win five.

"Everything we do today, apart from the fact that we have previously ignored the buying process, is around working with those who are still in the funnel. Eventually there are only 5 left in. 95 have leaked out and we plan nothing around the 95 and everything around the 5.

"The money is in how we deal with the 95. How quickly can we catch them when they leak, incubate them, and recycle them back into the funnel as fast as we can?"

Sue's attempt at drawing what they had discussed was not likely to win any design prizes.

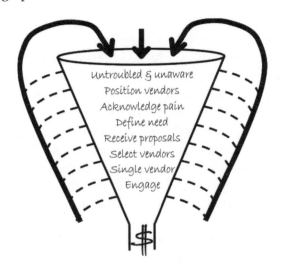

She repeated the notion she had taken from this exchange. "The money is in how quickly and effectively we can recycle leakage."

"And stop the leakage in the first place, surely," argued Kyle helpfully.

"Sure."

"Well, is it, though Sue?" Warren asked. "I disagree. You can't stop prospects from leaking. I think the second bit is about how successfully you cause some to progress, rather than trying to sweat all of them. Brett, you know what your sales people are like. Some of them just keep working the same opportunities which everyone except them seems to know are dead, when they should move on."

Sue picked up the thread. "OK, so we're saying that our success will come from how well we cause prospects to progress from one stage to the next in their buying cycle, and how well we deal with the failure."

It felt right. It also felt like about 10.15 and after agreeing they had covered enough for the day, the meeting quickly disbanded.

From: Sue Hunt

Sent: Monday, 18 March

To: Graham Chase
Brett Marsden
Kyle Hoffman
Warren Jackson
Sarah Martin

Subject: Recycling leakage

Team

Another great session today, thanks. Next week we're going to look at measures again. I want to try to get a handle on rates of leakage and recycling next week, so bring your left brains.

And I'll bring the coffee!

Best, Sue

The past reveals the future

During the week, Sue reviewed the goaling of sales people with Brett. She was reminded of how important measurement was to sales people, and the clear and direct link between goaling and behaviour. Brett also reminded her though of their now-shared belief that the inputs shape the output. They selected three potentially viable paths, but agreed to not conclude their approach until after the planning workshops had delivered some clarity on the outputs they needed.

On Monday, Sue returned the team's attention to measurement. "Last week we discovered the effect of recycling, and agreed that the focus is on causing progression, rather than trying to stop the leakage, and then recycling the leakage as quickly and effectively as we can.

"Today I want to re-explore measures to see if there is some impact this can have on leakage and recycling. No one had any specific homework on this, so let's capture collective thoughts, maybe starting with a brainstorm. Sarah, you want to do the honours?"

"What stage do you want to work first, Sue?"

"Maybe let's start with what we know can be measured today."

Sarah was a good facilitator and got them thinking. Each suggestion led to others, and the team had pretty much exhausted the options once she stopped. They removed duplications, and were left with a list of factors which they were confident were already measured in one sense or another. The list had a few of Warren's suggestions of a few weeks ago, but no longer included management measures – they were more interested in measures of leakage and recycling.

She redrew the list for clarity:

Measured today, or easily added
- Calls to get a meeting
- First presentations to get an opportunity to propose
- Proposals to get a deal
- Brand awareness

Sue felt they had exhausted the line of thought, but on looking at their list, felt they had produced little of any use. "This isn't taking us anywhere. It's clear that current measurement approaches won't help us. Let's let it sit for now. If we were trying to measure our progress against the customer journey, which stages could we measure without too much work?"

After a little dialogue, the team agreed that:
- *Untroubled and unaware* is easy – it's everyone in the target market
- *Position vendors* and acknowledge pain can be tested with research
- *Define need* could be measured with research, but is probably best determined by the sales force keeping records
- *Receive proposals* and all stages after that are already measured
- Nothing is measured for recycling as they don't do it today.

Again, Sue was happy that they had worked the issue well, but wasn't happy about how useful it had been. "So where does that take us? I feel we're flapping in the breeze a bit."

They all agreed. Sue tried to eke some value from the work. "If we had these measures though, could we model our probable success based on past success?"

"Sure we could, as long as we had confidence in our ability to keep meeting the success rates." Warren knew that predictions would be only as useful as the reliability of the assumptions. "We'd have to get the measures anyway, and not just for modelling. If we can measure the early stages of the funnel, we can fix the problem of the sales forecast being too late. If we know, for example that we are short on prospects who acknowledge their pain, then we will probably end up short on proposals six months later. So we have to sort it out."

Sue wanted to move the conversation back to modelling. "Alright. So, Graham, how hard would it be to build this?"

"Easy, but dangerous." They could tell Graham was ready to share another of his gems. "I spoke to a friend at System House, and they use a process pretty similar to our funnel. They draw it differently, something more like a step diagram, but the idea of a progressive leakage is the same, even if they don't use that language. Came from a course they had Mary Molloy run for them a few years back. He gave me a copy of the book she and her husband Mike wrote called *The Buck Starts Here*. It seems we are not as original as we might have thought.

"Anyway, their model puts equal emphasis on the time it takes to progress from one stage to the next as they do on the success rate of that stage."

"So what's the value of that Graham? If we aren't sure how well we can measure leakage, why do we focus on delay also?" Warren remained cautious about building complex models on top of flimsy assumptions.

Graham continued. "Let's say it took a prospect eight weeks to acknowledge their pain, and five weeks to define their need, that's thirteen weeks, or one quarter. The effect of this delay of just those two stages would mean that revenue in the first quarter would be exactly zero because all the prospects would be pushed out to the following quarter before we even allow for the other stages.

"So, if we built a simple model to deal with leakages, we'd be kidding ourselves. We have to allow for the lag effect as well."

Sue persisted. "So, can you do it?"

"You'd have to ask Warren. IT reports to him, and I reckon this is a systems challenge, not a process one."

Warren was reluctant. "Look, it can be done, but it's not as simple as it looks. Let me have one of the guys look at it during the week and I'll see what he comes up with. What about this process used at System House, Graham. Do we need to look at that?"

"I think so, Jeff swears by it, and there seems to be a lot of parallels with what we are trying to do."

Sarah volunteered to read *The Buck Starts Here* over the weekend and write a one-page summary for the others.

Sue was tired. "OK, modelling aside, and subject to looking further at this other process, what have we achieved?"

Graham, as always, had a good sense of perspective. "Sue, our emphasis has been on modelling and benchmarking and estimating success rates. What we have not discussed, but I think emerges from this way of thinking, is that there are some of the progressions best achieved by Marketing, some by Sales, and some, like incubation, that need both. Maybe a bit of back and forth also. I think we can have Sales and Marketing working together."

"Nice," Sue replied, "But we agreed we weren't setting out to fix the problems, but to work out a way to earn more customers. Have we done that?"

Kyle volunteered: "If we choose our tactics well in the first place, then yes. At least we have a framework for choosing our tactics now."

"And I suppose we also now have a way of working out if these tactics are doing their job." *Good on Warren*, Sue thought. *The numbers man.*

He continued. "It would be good if we could benchmark against others also." Then, leaning across to Sarah in a mock whisper, "Hey Sarah, maybe we should help you write that book so other companies use this process and we can benchmark against them?"

They chuckled, but agreed benchmarking would be a logical next step.

Sue wrapped for the day. "Guys, let's park it for now because there are a few loose ends left from today that I'd like to reflect on before bringing this to a head before next week. I'll give this some thought and shoot out an email later today."

From:	Sue Hunt
Sent:	Monday, 25 March
To:	Graham Chase
	Brett Marsden
	Kyle Hoffman
	Warren Jackson
	Sarah Martin
Subject:	Modelling

Team,

Today was a bit of a wander. Nonetheless, I believe we took a lot from it. We have a number of outstanding issues to resolve:

- Segmentation based on the problem;
- A review by Sarah of *The Buck Starts Here;*
- Refinement of the customer journey;
- What to measure.

I'm going to suggest we skip our next two workshops. I have a Board meeting, and we'll need some time to chase some of these to ground anyway.

I'll suggest Sarah takes ownership of the first three of these outstanding items, and that Warren retains ownership of measurement.

Our next workshop then will be Monday 15 April. I think we're only going to know if we have anything useful by then if we test it out. I'd like to develop our plan for new customer acquisition using our new process. Therefore we need to give this a whole day. I know we have other work on as well, but for this workshop particularly, we need to give this some time. New customers are our number one priority as a company, and I want it to be your number one priority personally also. I'm open, as always, to discussion on this.

Kyle and Sarah, can we meet Thursday some time to discuss the planning for this new market? I'd like you to take stewardship of the planning process.

Best, Sue

Anchors aweigh

The team

The management team had worked well together. The jibes remained mostly friendly, and the contributions were sufficiently diverse that Sue allowed herself to think they were covering the right number of bases as they went.

Brett and Kyle had each separately spoken with Sue after receiving her email of Monday. They were keen to be a part of the team and to help make changes, but were concerned about the time commitment. A full day per week was a bit over the top and they doubted their ability to meet their day-to-day commitments.

Sue hadn't really expected the pushback. After arguing the importance that they make this change together, she found herself getting tougher than she had intended. She reminded them that their day-to-day activities were not cutting it, and that they could pretty much skip these and there would be little effect on short term revenues. Neither Brett nor Kyle appreciated the suggestion, and Sue regretted throwing this at them. She suspected it was valid, but counselled herself that the coming weeks would chew up a lot of time and until they identified things the organisation would stop doing, the team would get busier before it got better.

Although Sue's brief when she took on the role was to teach the organisation how to better understand the customer, and to leverage that understanding, she had not imagined that this would require inventing a new approach to earning customers. *Have we really invented something, or have we just brought a number of established truths together?* It suited Sue to take the latter view, as she wanted the staff to see the company as one which best understood the customer, not one which invented neat processes.

Nonetheless, they had covered a lot of ground in the two months since the problems became clear, and the six months since Sue started. A summary to the team was in order:

From:	Sue Hunt
Sent:	Wednesday, 27 March
To:	Graham Chase
	Brett Marsden
	Kyle Hoffman
	Warren Jackson
	Sarah Martin
Subject:	Anchors aweigh

In three weeks we will again meet to develop our plan for new customer acquisition. I would like to bring together in a complete form what I believe we have learned over the last two months working on this as a team. You have all contributed equally, and I hope take equal ownership of what we have achieved.

There are four key questions I seek to address in this note:

1.   What have we learned?
2.   Have we dealt with the four anchors?
3.   Will this accelerate customer acquisition?
4.   What's next?

I see the answers as follows:

What have we learned?

1.   We chose the customer journey rather than the selling process as the framework for our thinking. Prospects start untroubled and unaware, and along the way they have some early discussions, acknowledge that they have pain, define a need, deal with vendors then engage one of them.

2.   We agreed that our strategies and tactics should be shaped around helping prospects to progress along this journey. I can tell you that in my experience as a buyer, neither HardBits nor its competitors had any idea of how I bought.

3.   We discovered that as prospects progress along their journey, some leak out.

4.   We identified that this leakage was so great, that we needed to have specific programs to recycle the leaked prospects back into the funnel.

5.   We decided it was better to focus on causing progression and recycling the leakage than to try to stop or diminish the leakage, otherwise we spend all of our time sweating over a few deals that might already be dead.

6.   We identified that we should split our target market into segments based around their attitude to the problems they face, rather than their industry or other approaches we have typically taken to segmentation in the past.

7.   We agreed that lag is just as important as leakage, and that if we can predict and measure them with any accuracy, we will be able to model our probable success.

8.   We agreed that if we get others to do it as well, we can benchmark our success rates to know if we are doing well or poorly. This will be hard, because I saw no evidence when I was at DHM that vendors are into benchmarking their Sales and Marketing.

We discussed many more subjects, but I feel these are the key out-takes. I believe that the aggregate of this learning is that we have assembled a number of proven truths, rather than created a wholly new approach. Nothing in the above is 100% new, and much of it can be seen in action in other companies. Nonetheless, I have not seen these views assembled fully anywhere before, and believe that if we are breaking new ground anywhere, it is in the assembly rather than creation of this learning.

Have we dealt with the four anchors?

You will recall that I was not keen to set about specifically solving the problems because I wanted us to focus on earning customers, not solving problems. Naturally, though, we needed an approach that would address the constraints those anchors represent. I will address each separately:

Sales and Marketing on different planets

Whilst the workshops have brought the leaders of each function together, this is a temporary benefit, and is not deep within the organisation. The more systemic benefit will come from having a single framework for planning used by both functions, and by then selecting which parts of the journey, or our recycling, is owned by each function, or jointly. Perhaps more concisely, we have the makings of a remedy to this, but will need to retain focus for there to be any sustained gain.

The buying process ignored

We have fundamentally turned this on its head. We now build our processes around the buyer and his/her journey.

Arbitrary tactics

In the upcoming planning workshop, I want you to disregard all current tactics, and identify and select whichever tactics will best cause the progression we seek along the buying process. Some of our current tactics will be reinstated, others will be discarded, and we may find we introduce some new tactics. Tactics must be 'tasked' narrowly with causing this progression. If we do this, we have very purposeful tactics, and we choose them well. I consider this anchor addressed.

Our indicators tell us nothing

This will be the hardest of all. If we plan the whole buyer journey, and predict their rates of progression (both lag and leakage), then we must also measure lag & leakage. We probably should benchmark them; internally at first, and then externally. If we measure them well, we'll know how we're progressing well before we see any movement in the sales forecast. As with anchor number 1, I feel we have the strategy for an answer, but must work on execution.

In summary, two of the four anchors ('ignoring the buying process' and 'arbitrary tactics') have been addressed, and for the other two we have the concept right, but must execute well.

Will this accelerate customer acquisition?

I have 100% confidence, and 0% proof. Our new approach is more complete in its scope, and more aligned to the buyer in its design.

As a former buyer, I believe that this approach would have completely changed my view of HardBits. Importantly, it would also have brought our two organisations closer as we'd have been working on more aligned activities.

As suggested earlier, although this approach is simply an assembly of established best practice, we are breaking new ground in pulling all these changes together and will not be able to rely on others paving the way. I am convinced we are on the right track, and am committed to supporting you as you set out to prove it.

What's next?

1.   The customer journey itself might need further refinement. I feel the first use of this notion will test it and probably produce some change.

2.   We need greater clarity around problem-based or behaviour-based segmentation. Although Sarah is doing some work on this over the next fortnight, I feel this too will change in its first use.

3.   Until we agree the buying stages and set predictions for them, we'll not know what we need to measure. I am sure though, that this will prove to be a major task in itself and will take several attempts to get right.

Best, Sue

The Board

Sue knew that the Board would be expecting some clarity on the results of their work on addressing the four anchors. Revenues had not declined in the March quarter, but they hadn't increased either. Sue was lucky to have a team able to keep the ship on course without her daily intervention. Her job really was to identify and effect change, not to maintain the momentum. *All the more pressure on me to sell them on where we got to,* she mused. *So, build our little voyage of discovery or lay it out straight?* Sue opted for a basic Board paper, distributed for reading beforehand, and would field their questions on the day.

Sue condensed the 'Anchors Aweigh' email to her staff and used this as the basis of the Board briefing. It took her a few goes to remove the jargon that had crept into the language between team members. Her cover note to the Board concluded confidently:

> I am confident that the successful adoption of this approach will deliver measurable improvements to our ability to earn new business, and have committed the team to a planning program which will see us ready to execute from 1 July.

Something in the way she had been forced to articulate this for the Board paper added a little clarity for Sue. She made a few notes to include in the team briefing meeting next Monday.

The Board whistled through the standing items in their usual efficient manner, and turned to the last item on the agenda – Sue's update on the four anchors.

"So, Sue, you missed something off the Board briefing." Lars often had such an expressionless face, Sue still found it hard to read him. "What do you want to do and what decision are you asking the Board to make? What budget do you need? What resources do you need?"

"Nothing Lars. I don't need additional budget, I have the right team, and I don't need the Board."

"So, are you dismissing us? Are we no longer needed?"

"Oh, sorry, I didn't mean it like that." Lars was smiling and Sue knew he had got her. "It's just that although I feel this change will produce real improvements, it is not one which requires me to change resources or add costs. In fact I feel we'll end up doing fewer things in the end. I just need you to back me, that's all."

"I thought we made the decision to back you in July last year Sue." Lars was still smiling. So was Sue.

The road and the rubber

From: Sue Hunt

Sent: Wednesday, 10 April

To: Graham Chase
                 Brett Marsden
                 Kyle Hoffman
                 Warren Jackson
                 Sarah Martin

Subject: Monday's workshop

On Monday, we have our first full-day planning session for earning new customers. Just as our design of the new approach required your collective experience, so this plan development needs to be a joint initiative of the whole management team. Kyle has asked Sarah to join the meeting as facilitator again. She has proposed the following agenda, which I propose we adopt.

15 April	Strategy review
22 April	Positioning
29 April	The buyer's journey
6 May	Lags and leakages
13 May	Tactics
20 May	Measurement and benchmarks
27 May	Plan for execution

That will give us just one month to prepare anything necessary for execution 1 July. I am aware that you already have lots on your plates, and therefore propose:

– We meet every Monday until 1pm for the next seven weeks (we had originally said all day).

– However, rather than let our timetable slip, we keep going each day until we conclude the agenda item. We'll endeavour to finish by 1pm, but I suggest you make no plans for the afternoons.

– If we fail to conclude an item at a reasonable hour, or if anything else crops up we'll have to allocate additional time during the week, or even weekends if necessary.

This all sounds a little draconian, but it is better to acknowledge this as a major undertaking now than let it creep up on us. Make any

> contingencies you need to so that you can be clear for these dates, and call or come see me if any of this presents major challenges for you.
>
> Best, Sue

Sue had sent this email before 8am. By 5pm she'd heard nothing, and didn't know whether to treat the absence of any calls or emails as a sign that each of her team was committed to the task, were busy, or that they were annoyed with her for this impost.

From:	Graham Chase
Sent:	Wednesday, 10 April
To:	Sue Hunt
	Brett Marsden
	Kyle Hoffman
	Warren Jackson
	Sarah Martin
Subject:	Re: Monday's workshop

I'll take a standing brief for the coffees.

Cheers, Graham

With *that* question now clearly answered, Sue left for home.

Strategy review

"Good morning caffeine hounds," Sue began chirpily.

"You have in front of you a copy of the agenda per my email last week. You've also got on the table a copy of the research reports Kyle and Sarah circulated last week. We'll perhaps need to refer to them later. Graham has provided some capacity predictions, and Warren has done some revenue analysis by customer. I think these will prove handy today. I suggest you resist the temptation to read them now, as we'll get lost right off the bat if we do.

"So, Ms Facilitator, the floor's yours."

Sarah flashed her first slide up. It was the seven-week agenda. Sarah knew they had all seen it, but it had seemed like a good idea when she had prepared the slide set on Friday. It appeared a little less necessary now, so she moved on quickly.

"As you know, today is about capturing what we assume to be the key aspects of our strategy. I don't imagine much of this will change. The purpose of working through this though is that the core strategy operates as such a strong foundation, that it will not be good enough if we are only partially clear. So..." Sarah moved to her next slide, "these are the topics I propose we cover today." She read through them providing a little commentary by way of explanation for each:

- Situation (what do we think is going on)?
- To whom (that is, who do we wish to target)?
- Through whom (that is, what channel – direct or indirect or both – do we use to reach them)?
- With what (what do we offer them - this covers product, price and packaging)?
- Objectives (how much of what do we plan to sell)?

–   Competition (who will we compete with and how are we posi-
    tioned to do this)?

"Shouldn't we start with objectives Sarah?" asked Warren.

"Normally, sure. By objectives at this stage I really mean just
the revenue objectives, Warren. They are so influenced by who we
choose to target, that I think it's easier to first identify the target.
Are you OK with that, Sue?"

Sarah threw it back to Sue as it had been her idea in the first
place. "Sure." It wasn't an important point, so Warren let it pass.

Situation

Sarah's third slide was a little more interesting.

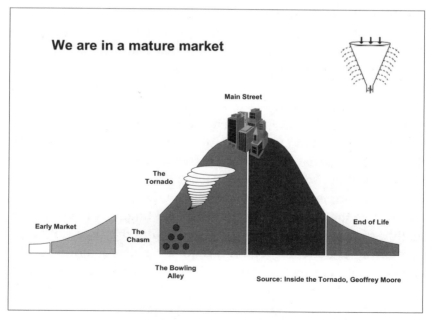

"Some of you would be familiar with the idea of the product lifecycle. This is a variant on the one we have been using for a while.
It's by a guy called Geoffrey Moore and better explains how buyers

behave. Anyway, to skip the lesson in theory, I put it up only to seek agreement that the markets in which our products play is mature, and that most of our potential buyers have already bought, and that we are really trying to sack their current supplier and replace them. All agreed?"

There was a little banter about what all the symbols meant, but Sarah was clear enough in her objective of getting them to agree the maturity that she avoided going into an effusive sales pitch for Moore's theory, argued in *Crossing the Chasm* and *Inside the Tornado*. Sarah was a fan of Moore's theories, but knew this was not the time for a detailed explanation. *Inside the Tornado* had become the bible for technology companies around the world, and she saw no reason why the principles didn't apply equally to their business.

But Warren would have none of it. "Sorry Sarah, you're going to have to give us a refresher. We all know about product lifecycle, but this looks a little different."

Sarah drew breath and began – firstly the classic theory and then Geoffrey Moore's twist. She explained that early in the life of a new product there were few customers. Typically those that did buy were somewhat visionary. Then the product's reputation and visibility encouraged others to embrace it, until acceptance grew, eventually peaked and then declined. Some buyers though, were slow to adopt and did not buy until quite late in the piece, earning the name 'laggards.' The diagram showed volume of buyers (the vertical axis) over time (horizontal axis).

Moore argued that with discontiguous change (stop start change like the car replacing the horse and buggy), there was normally a difficult period when marketers found they had run out of market rather suddenly, before eventually rising again along the normal curve. He described this sudden slow period after the early market as a chasm, and explained that after all the early adopters had bought, the next group were pragmatists who typically did not buy until they could see someone 'just like me' buy.

Sarah's dissertation was clear and relatively jargon-free. She looked at her colleagues to see if they were happy to move on.

Then the switch - Sarah had done her homework. "OK, if we agree we have a very mature market, let's see what Moore would suggest by way of strategy. I throw these up as input for now."

Strategy for a mature market

- Buyer is the end user
- Focus is on finding new uses
- Value proposition is "fully meeting your needs"
- Segmentation is horizontal, or new small niches
- Product is complete, and maybe enhance for niches
- Pricing is market, (or higher if we have a "+ one" proposition)
- Alliances only if pursuing niches
- Move beyond the competition
- Narrow services
- Our advantage is operational efficiency + customer intimacy
- Key disciplines are convenience, marketing communication & margin management

Graham cleared his throat. "It looks like your Mr Moore has our strategy all sorted Sarah. Can I go home now?"

"I wasn't suggesting we don't have to work through strategy on our own, only that there are some proven approaches that we should be mindful of."

"Relax Sarah, I was complimenting you. This is good input, and looks complete. Although I have to confess I understand about 10% of it."

"OK, ah, thanks." *When in doubt, play it straight,* thought Sarah. She resumed. "Again, these are only inputs." Then in response to Graham's comment about understanding 10% suggested, "Let's look at the six aspects of strategy we have on the agenda, and use this as a guide as we go. OK?" This time Sarah wanted their agreement to the process, and waited until they had all nodded or confirmed. She knew that many of the terms were undefined, but intended addressing each as they wove their way into the discussion around strategy.

To whom

"What is the market?" Sarah asked.

It was meant to be a rhetorical question, but Kyle answered anyway. "Isn't the market segment horizontal according to that slide Sarah?" Kyle was feeling a little upstaged by his protégé. "But remember our discussion about problems? We agreed then that segmenting by problems was more meaningful for us, didn't we?"

"Yes, Moore is suggesting we segment horizontally, and yes, problems are horizontal. That is everyone has them, not just one industry. So, who do we want to target?" Sarah again looked at Sue, knowing that she had firm views on this, but Sue was clearly going to let the others contribute to this discussion.

Brett broke the silence. "I assume we are talking non-customers, yeah? And some sub-section of them for a start, yeah? OK, well my guys are already talking to those who want to switch. I reckon we focus on the untroubled and unaware."

Sue was delighted Brett had jumped to the same conclusion so quickly, and wanted to cement this view quickly. "Great idea Brett. Everyone OK with that?"

Warren, conscientious as always, didn't like the speed with which they arrived at the answer. "Didn't we have an open item on segmentation Sue? How did we resolve that?"

Sue deferred. "Sarah, you and Kyle and I worked on this together. Maybe you could update the other three."

Kyle might have answered, but Sarah had the floor, so jumped in quickly. "Sure. We liked the idea of buyer behaviour, but feel that 'attitude to problem' is a good proxy for it, and it is *much* easier and cheaper to work out who sits in which bucket early on if we take this approach. We decided 'attitude to the problem' was our best segmentation approach."

Brett sat back. "Is this someone within the company, or the company as a whole? Do we wander around looking for a bloke with a forehead without creases and run an IQ test on him?"

"Well," Graham smiled at Brett's visualisation of the untroubled and unaware buyer. "It would be the end-user according to your Mr Moore, wouldn't it Sarah?"

"Right."

"But that's not who we sell to," Brett countered. "The Manufacturing departments all insist we deal with Procurement."

Graham looked directly at Brett. "Is that perhaps why we find it hard to break in? I mean if the Procurement department have instructions to buy Plastix, why would they change to us? Surely that decision would come from Manufacturing?"

"Or Marketing?" It was Kyle's turn to counter.

"Excuse me?" asked Graham, playing no games at all.

"Think about it. Marketing decides to make a new product, or some new packaging. They are the guys who are going to have a new need. They will of course go to Manufacturing to work out how to make it, but the agent of change for these people might be the end-users: Marketing, Sales, even Finance."

"It'd require some training to get our reps to call on those guys," offered Brett, "And they could easily waste days trying to find out who to talk to."

Sue sensed this was not the time to get bogged down in implementation details. "Let's not solve the 'how' just now OK? Are you comfortable that we are probably talking to an end-user department in a company that currently sees no need to switch?"

"OK."

Through whom?

Sarah again restated the meaning of the next topic. "What channels will be used?" She was keen to regain her rhythm, though, so quickly continued. "So, if we target the end-users of the untroubled and unaware, which channel do we use?"

"It has to be direct doesn't it?" Brett was hardly going to consider any alternative. "I mean, we use direct reps now, and the tornado man seems to agree."

"But what about skills?" asked Kyle. "If our reps are not up to selling to the end-user, maybe we should consider a channel."

Sue offered a mid-point. "I don't think a skill gap is a good reason to change the channel strategy, but do we need to supplement it? Well, maybe not supplement it, but perhaps Marketing could take on more of the role. You know - do the fishing around to find out which end-user is ready to move?"

"We could," Kyle offered, "But that might be expensive research. What if we did some marketing to get a few creases in their forehead? Sort of warm them up for Sales and get them a little less 'untroubled'?"

"Or both?" asked Sue. "Can we do some base profiling so we know who the *untroubled and unaware* are, then warm them until one sticks his head above the trench for Brett's guys to engage with?"

"That makes sense." Kyle seemed happy. "It's not cheap, but neither is having sales people meandering around looking for the *untroubled and unaware*."

"OK, I'm happy. Let's keep going," chimed in Brett, always keen to get on with things.

With what?

Sue began. "Now, Graham, you said in an earlier workshop that we don't tend to change our product much between segments. If you knew we were targeting end-users in companies that don't know they have a problem, does this still hold true?"

"Sure."

Sarah looked for more. "What if we said that plastic beads might be a complete product for Manufacturing, but Marketing need prototypes and short-run moulded plastic to prove their concept both to the market and to Manufacturing?"

"OK, I get you. Sue, do you remember how Frank got no support for wanting to buy that small job run manufacturer? Maybe it was a good idea after all. Although they are unprofitable, and likely to stay that way, and we probably couldn't get them to profitability ourselves, they might be a cheap way to buy short run capability for new proofs of concept."

Now we're cooking, thought Sue. "Our base product doesn't change, but what we are offering is a way to create or prove new products. That certainly gets us closer to our customers. What about pricing though? How can we get our margins up?"

She answered her own question. "By not selling HardBits as a bead supplier, but as a product development partner. Eventually we'll get pushed down to commodity prices, but maybe for a while with each new customer we can enjoy higher pricing by not packaging this up as a bead deal at all."

"So, value pricing," said Sarah quickly.

"Isn't value pricing code for premium pricing?" Warren was on his anti-jargon bandwagon.

"No, it is pricing in each market according to how much they value the offering." Sarah prided herself on being able to answer these questions, not realising that Warren was having a dig at her use of jargon rather than seeking an education. She persisted anyway. "Innovators would value the total outcome highly, whereas once they get momentum, we are back to basic beads and commodity prices."

Sue looked to Brett. "Are your guys capable of selling such a story?"

"Some, but with a deal like that we're talking about needing to establish a broad set of linkages between their hierarchy and ours anyway. My guys can get a deal like this to the table, then it's up to a whole host of people, mainly us in this room to be frank, to pull it across the line. So let me turn it around: Are *we* up to it?"

"I think we can cope," said Graham being dry, but just as excited as the others.

Helen, Sue's PA, turned up with a platter of sandwiches and another of fruit, some drinks and a fresh pot of coffee. No-one dared tell Helen they'd prefer espressos from across the road, but Sue made a note to discuss it with Helen before next Monday. Their morning coffees had set a new standard.

Objectives

"OK, are we set to go again?" Sarah asked.

The chatter over lunch had done nothing to quell their enthusiasm. The team was working well together.

"If we are targeting the end-user, probably Sales or Marketing in *untroubled and unaware* companies, using Marketing to profile them and warm them up, then our own reps to get a deal on the table and the broader company to close it, and we're offering a way for these companies to innovate with plastics, how much can we realistically sell?"

"42," volunteered Graham. Not everyone was a *Hitchhiker's Guide to the Galaxy* fan like Graham. Perhaps they didn't get the specific meaning of his joke, but it sort of worked anyway.

"Yeah, sorry. It was a bit like that." Sarah hadn't lost her momentum. "Really though, how big do we think that market is, and how much of it do you think we could get?"

Kyle was doodling on a pad in front of him, but following every word. "You won't get any market data on this because *untroubled and unaware* for us are somebody else's satisfied customers."

Sarah had a go at answering her own question. "If we are only 10% of the market, it's almost 90% isn't it? Or, what if we developed some sort of profiling which said we only want companies that are bigger than X or smaller than Y, or had an organisational bias towards innovation, or some other filters, how big then?"

"Wow Sarah, too fast." *Warren, the conscientious* to the rescue again. "You're talking about a whole bunch of homework to answer that one."

"Maybe," offered Graham. "Surely we tweak the filters to give us the result we want. I believe we are talking about maybe 20% of the market, which means maybe 1000 companies all up. I'd like to see us get maybe 300 of these from such a campaign."

"Up front or over time?" asked Brett, concerned.

"Oh Christ, Brett! Over time. Some of these would take years to get across, but some would come faster. Give it three years and I'd like to see 300 come across."

"And probably some sort of ramp up?" offered Kyle helpfully.

"Ah yes, the inevitable parabolic growth curve?" Graham had seen too many optimistic presentations that argued easy targets early on and crazy, unachievable growth in the later years.

"Well, maybe." Brett wasn't keen to see them agree to an unrealistic goal. "But you'd agree there would be some sort of ramp wouldn't you?"

"Sure."

Competition

Sarah donned her facilitator's hat once more. "So who is going to get in our way?"

"Plastix, GRM, EnviroPlas, EuroNue." Brett counted them off on his fingers. "And probably even Sartle. All the usual suspects."

"OK, now indulge me a little, forget about strengths and weaknesses. For *any one* of those companies, what would they have to get right if they were trying to tackle the *untroubled and unaware*?"

Brett was straight off the mark. "We'd have to increase our brand awareness for a start."

"Not *us* Brett," Sarah chided. "What would *any one* of these companies, us included, have to get right?"

"Brett's right though Sarah," offered Kyle. "Brand awareness is one of them. Probably competitive product is another. I'd suggest an ability to innovate would be key also."

"Whoa there Kyle, I can't write that fast." Sarah was scribbling furiously, but apparently not furiously enough.

They continued for almost half an hour before agreeing the list of Critical Success Factors. Sarah drew a matrix of the Critical Success Factors and the companies. "You must have known I was going to matrix you sooner or later." It felt better when she had a go at herself than when the others did.

"Now, we need to debate who is well positioned to meet each of these Critical Success Factors, and who is not." They continued on until 3.30 debating who was stronger than another on each of the Critical Success Factors. Sarah had a preferred model for doing this, and found herself having a low-yield argument with Brett over process. Sarah got a little caught up in the theory, and Brett niggled because his tolerance for the process was low. A little frustrating overall, but they eventually reached consensus on their competitive position

5 is strongest 1 is weakest	HardBits	Plastix	GRM	EnviroPlas	EuroNue	Sartle	Average
Reputation as an innovator	4	2	1	3	2	2	2.3
Ability to assist new development	2	3	2	2	3	3	2.5
Competitive base product	3	4	3	2	2	1	2.5
Ability to engage with the buyer	2	3	2	4	3	2	2.7
Capacity to serve new market	3	3	2	2	2	4	2.7
Total	14	15	10	13	12	12	13

"Sarah, I suggest we need a decent break," said Sue looking every bit as tired as she felt. "Energy is running very low, and I for one need a bio-break."

"But we're done Sue, we just need to wrap up."

Sue insisted. "OK guys, let's take a 15 minute leg stretch then and come back to wrap up. In fact, why not make it 30, and maybe I can coax Helen into getting some decent coffee. Standard order all 'round?"

"Well done Sue. See you at 4 then."

They were all back well within the 30 minutes, so Sarah kicked off while Helen was still passing around the coffees to the "Well done" and "Thanks" of the crew.

"I probably jumped the gun a bit. Given we know where we stand competitively, what are we going to do about it?"

Brett turned to Graham, passed the sugar, and asked, "How serious were you about buying that short-run manufacturer Graham?"

"We shouldn't make that an assumption in the strategy, but it's fair to say we need to get a jobbing capability."

Kyle repeated his earlier call. "We'd also need to change our brand perception, but I think we're dealing with that next week."

Sarah re-explained what she meant by her question. "I'm thinking competitive strategy here. What do we do to change our competitive position? Attack, flank, surround?"

"Sarah, you're a closet aggressor," said Kyle, meaning well by his comment.

"Yeah, right. I didn't think it was *that* closet. But anyway, how do we want to change this?"

This little 'aside' turned out to be a major discussion, and took them through until 6, but the energy remained high this time. The walls were covered in butcher's paper attached with blue-tack.

Sarah slumped in a chair. "So, is that it?"

She again answered her own question. "I think since we're all a bit tired, why don't I take the task of writing this up and circulating. Maybe you could just help me now though by agreeing the key points." She talked, wrote and listed simultaneously, and did a good job of summarising the key out-takes from the day.

- *Untroubled and unaware*, mainly the end-user.
- Marketing to profile and then warm up, direct Sales to get a deal on the table, then a broad company-wide engagement.
- Complete solution for innovation. Value pricing – premium for innovators, commodity as they mature.
- 300 companies from a target of 1000, over three years.

– HardBits needs to change something major to win. Especially need to re-skill our sales force and find some way to include short runs as a part of new product innovation for clients.

When the contributions subsided, she asked again, "Is that about it?"

"Well done Sarah," said Graham. "You did a good job today."

"Hear, hear," the others offered.

"Gee, thanks, guys." She batted her eyelids in mock coyness, which was very out of character, but allowed her to deal with the unwanted attention. Sarah was not one who enjoyed compliments.

From: Sarah Martin

Sent: Tuesday, 16 April

To: Sue Hunt
Graham Chase
Brett Marsden
Kyle Hoffman
Warren Jackson

Subject: Strategy

Hi all

Thanks for your perseverance yesterday. See the attached page. It's a little rough, but I think it is pretty close to what we agreed. I've also taken a stab at the numbers.

Let me know if you want any changes before next Monday.

Regards, Sarah

To whom

We will target the Marketing and Sales Directors of the 1000 companies who are currently using plastics as a key component of their product development, but lack the ability to innovate substantially in-house.

Through whom

We will use our marketing competencies to profile the above companies (including name and all contact details), then to warm these prospects before Sales involvement. Our direct sales force will be trained to identify defined needs from these prospects and to bring a deal to the table. Sales will own closure, but we expect the broader organisation to be involved in an innovation sale.

With what

Our standard product, together with a product innovation team, and a yet-to-be-acquired short-run facility will be packaged as a new product innovation partnership. Pricing will be set individually for each company based on the value we believe they will gain from this innovation, but will be no less than base price + 20%.

Competitive strategy

5 is strongest 1 is weakest	HardBits	Plastix	GRM	EnviroPlas	EuroNue	Sartle	Average
Reputation as an innovator	4	2	1	3	2	2	2.3
Ability to assist new development	2	3	2	2	3	3	2.5
Competitive base product	3	4	3	2	2	1	2.5
Ability to engage with the buyer	2	3	2	4	3	2	2.7
Capacity to serve new market	3	3	2	2	2	4	2.7
Total	14	15	10	13	12	12	13

HardBits is positioned as an innovator, but lacks the ability to assist new customers to innovate. We will form an innovation team from Manufacturing, and acquire some capability to produce short runs necessary for product innovation.

We will move past our competition. That is, we will seek to create our own position and not position off other vendors. We will not engage in competitive knock offs, but will retrain our sales force to set an agenda with prospects that leaves them only one option – HardBits.

Objectives

The effect of this new business drive will be to grow 20% revenues cumulative for three years before flattening out.

		New clients gained	New customers cumulative	Volume per client (tonnes)	New volume sold (tonnes)	Volume cumulative (tonnes)	Current volume sold (tonnes)	Price per tonne (A$)	Revenue (A$'000)
Year 1	Q1	0	0	300	0	0	10,000	$2,500	$25,000
	Q2	14	14	300	4,200	4,200	10,000	$2,500	$35,500
	Q3	16	30	300	4,800	9,000	10,000	$2,500	$37,000
	Q4	19	49	300	5,700	14,700	10,000	$2,500	$39,250
Year 2	Q1	21	70	300	6,300	21,000	10,000	$2,500	$40,750
	Q2	24	94	300	7,200	28,200	10,000	$2,500	$43,000
	Q3	28	122	300	8,400	36,600	10,000	$2,500	$46,000
	Q4	32	154	300	9,600	46,200	10,000	$2,500	$49,000
Year 3	Q1-4	146	300	300	43,800	90,000	40,000	$2,500	$209,500

From:	Sue Hunt
Sent:	Tuesday, 16 April
To:	Sarah Martin
CC:	Graham Chase
	Brett Marsden
	Kyle Hoffman
	Warren Jackson
Subject:	Re: Strategy

Sarah, well done – no changes needed.

All, see you Monday 8am. Helen has a surprise for us Monday. I'll get the coffees this time Graham.

Best, Sue

The analysis of Critical Success Factors had provided a useful assessment of HardBits' competitive position. If they were to be successful in pursuing this new, complacent market, they would need to become a different company. Different in perception, and different in reality. Sue knew that next week's workshop would be seen by Warren and Brett in particular, but probably Graham also, as a soft discussion. Sue knew it would be anything but soft.

Mind where you're sitting

The week provided Brett with another opportunity to debrief a losing tender. This time it was Dairy Fresh, the nation's largest milk supplier. The meeting was set with Aravind Singh, the Manufacturing Director, and Evan Walker, the Marketing Director.

"Frankly Brett, we gave it to the least conformant tender, but by far the best one." Evan took great delight in showing Brett the tender response, and the mock-up the winning bidder had provided of the solution they envisioned.

What annoyed Brett was that the winning bidder wasn't a manufacturer, but a creative packaging team from a design agency. He took solace from the notion that the design agency might still be able to be persuaded to use HardBits for the supply.

"Where you stand on a subject, depends on where you sit." Sue began once they had found their seats on Monday morning. "I know someone clever or famous said that, but I've given up trying to remember who it was. Anyway, I thought it might be a good place to start a positioning discussion. It talks to our position in the market, but also to your preconceptions about today's agenda."

"Sue, where I sit right now, is at the end of table without a coffee in my hand," Brett joked.

"You line them up and I'll knock them down Brett," said Sue, referring to Brett's unintended 'straight man' act. "You could not have set that up better if you had rehearsed it. Helen…"

Helen entered the room pushing a small trolley carrying pastries, plates, forks, cups, and …

"Ta dah!" announced Helen rather ceremoniously. She removed the cloth from the object in the middle of the tray to reveal a small espresso machine. Everyone applauded, enjoying both the drama and the thought of good coffee. Coffee had clearly become something of a trademark of this team, and Sue was pleased for them to bond over anything, even if it was a hot drink made from a mildly addictive drug.

It was one of those nifty machines that uses little pods of preground coffee, so it was only a few minutes before 'Barista Helen' had them equipped with cappuccinos, caffé lattés, espressos and smiles.

"Thank you, Helen," they chorused before she extracted herself from the meeting. Helen was not quite as fond of coffee as this lot were, but was pleased about the fuss the little ceremony over the coffee machine - which had been her idea - had generated.

"Now, to today," Sue broke in to their coffee-house mood. "I confess to having spent most of my working life confused about positioning. Sarah and Kyle have been doing some work over the last fortnight to educate me, and I am going to test my understanding by telling you what I now think positioning is. Kyle, Sarah, pull me up where you think I am not being clear.

"We have two positioning challenges. One is to get the company into shape to optimise our profit. The second is to manage how the market perceives us. Neither of these are marketing issues, they are company-wide issues. I see today as being critical, and I hope we can keep the energy up to the level we enjoyed last week. Sarah, the floor is yours."

"So, you heard the lady," said Sarah. "To keep it up, I'm going to spare you as much of the theory as I can, but am going to have to cover a bit. I'll try to keep this super relevant and jargon free, but please be patient with me.

"You may be familiar with a guy called Michael Porter. He is widely known for his five forces, but the real..."

Sue smiled as Sarah continued to background the team. We had been here before when Sue was doing her initial digging, but this time Sarah was on the right track. No discussions about value chains. Sarah did a good job of holding their attention to lay out Porter's framework for understanding and optimising profit.

"So, the bottom line is, if we want to enjoy profits greater than the average for our industry, then we have to adopt only one of the three strategies, and be strong enough to not get lost in the middle. The options again, are 'cost leadership' (where you sell the product for about the same as others, but it costs you less to make), 'differentiation' (where you make it for about the same cost, but sell it for more because customers value something about your product more) and 'focus' (where you take one of those two approaches to a sub-set of the market).

"So," said Kyle picking up the thread, "We're not the cost leader. Plastix has 25 - 30% of the market and clearly has scale economies that we and others don't enjoy. So that means we can't also be a cost leader right?"

"Right," Sarah responded. "My take on this has changed over the last fortnight of homework. I think what we are proposing to do is a differentiation strategy. That is, our offer could appeal to the entire market, not just a part of it, and we want to command a premium for our differences."

"Sarah," Warren cut into Sarah's flow uncharacteristically. "Where is this going? Aren't we retro-fitting labels to a strategy we have already agreed?"

Kyle went to get up, but Sarah beat him to it. "It's OK. Warren, you are right. That's exactly what we are doing. But for good reason. If we acknowledge that we are pursuing a differentiation strategy, then by default we are electing to not pursue a cost leadership or focus strategy.

"The implications of this decision are not insignificant. For example, it means we should constantly work to change our offering to make sure it is always worth the premium we want to charge. We are saying the market is commoditised, and that despite this, we are going to continue to charge a premium. That's a big call."

"OK." But Warren, clearly not convinced, then contradicted himself. "It also runs counter to why Frank McInroth is no longer here. I thought the Board had given up on silver bullets and wanted to focus on getting understanding its customers better."

The room fell into a quiet state, waiting for Sue to speak as was her right on a subject of such magnitude (her position), but it was Graham who broke the silence. "Our strategy under Frank was to change our core product to allow us to command a premium. Our strategy under Sue is to change the way we engage with customers, and the value we can bring (for example, innovation in their use of plastic), to allow us to command a premium. Similar, but also very different."

Sarah had not entirely picked up on the significance of Warren's comment about Frank and Sue, and continued to discuss the importance of the strategic positioning as if nothing had been said. "It also means that we must continue to serve a broader market rather than just the *untroubled and unaware*.

"The *untroubled and unaware* market is a new focus for us. But if we continue to serve a broader market, we should also be charging them a premium. Otherwise we would enjoy none of the benefits of these strategies.

If we don't charge the largest part of our target market a premium, we'll lose money. On the one hand we don't enjoy the lower cost that comes from volume like Plastix, and on the other hand don't get to enjoy the efficiencies others might get from focusing on only a small section of the market.

"It means, that something has to change from last week, because we remain lost in the middle, other than for the *untroubled and unaware*. That is, we are not the cost leader, choose not to benefit from a narrow focus, yet don't have the right to charge *all* of the market a premium. Lost in the middle…"

The impact of what Sarah had said was not lost on any of the team. Nor was it lost on Sarah herself. She had not been clear where she was taking the conversation, even though she had thought she was. By going through the basic logic of the three generic strategies, Sarah and the others realised they still had work to do left over from last week.

Fortunately, the resolution proved less taxing than the realisation.

Graham sensed Sarah was a bit out of puff, and took the floor for a while. "Why do we think customers will pay us a premium?" and then in answer to his own question, "Because we will help them innovate."

"I started this company, and I stood down as CEO when I realised that it had grown faster than I had. That didn't bother me because my passion has always been to make our product the very best it could be, so the chance to return to that focus was a welcome one. This value of product quality is central to all the processes we have in Manufacturing, and in the staff I have there.

"With one small twist, I can change everything. If we focus on making our customers' products the very best they can be, we retain the values I founded the company on, and still cherish, and yet earn the right to charge everyone a fair price for even our most basic products."

It was one of those rare moments when five people in a small room could clap loudly in appreciation of the performance of a sixth person, and not feel particularly stupid. They didn't clap, but the mood shifted as if they had.

Graham sensed he may have overplayed it, so as he sat down sought to break things up with a little pompous "So there," followed by a grin.

It worked.

"So, I think we are differentiated," Warren said simply. It was enough.

Kyle slumped in his chair in mock resignation. "I can't beat that Sue, so can we have a break so I can organise a show band and some performing seals?"

"Sure. When we get back from a leg stretch, we'll have lunch, and then Kyle is going to take us through positioning with the market."

Conversation at lunch was about kids, weekends, golf, and anything except work generally, or positioning specifically. It was as if none of them wanted to spoil the sanctity of their new clarity.

With the plates cleared, and coffee out of the way, Kyle took the floor.

"The second part of this positioning discussion is about how our brand is perceived in the minds of our target audience, rather than how the company is positioned structurally to optimise profit. I'm going to unashamedly follow Sarah's lead here. I want to give you just enough of the theoretical framework to get us all on the same page, and then move to the meat of the subject.

"I'll confess that until recently, my focus on branding has been based on what I now consider to be a valid view for consumer brands, many of which are already established, and perfectly invalid for business brands, most of which are not well known to the buyers.

"Our focus on changing how the market views us is relevant only for those who already know who we are. The process of holding a powerful position in the mind of a business buyer is as follows:

1. Work out what pigeonhole we want prospects and customers to put us in;
2. Get in the pigeonhole; and
3. When we are properly within the pigeonhole, worry about whether we are in the right part of it.

"This sounds pretty basic, but most of market positioning discussion in specialist publications and the business press generally goes straight to number three without covering the first two points.

"For example, the Manufacturing and Procurement staff of most of the *untroubled and unaware* don't have us in the pigeon-hole at all. That is, they don't all know us to be a 'plastics supplier.' The Marketing and Sales staff of these same companies, don't even care that there is a pigeonhole called plastics suppliers. Whereas our customers know that there is such a pigeonhole, know that we are in it, and have a clear view about what part of that pigeonhole we occupy.

"See the difference?"

"I do, but I don't see what to do with this." Warren was happy to continue to play straight man to the Kyle and Sarah show.

"OK," said Kyle taking up the challenge, "Now to move from theory to practice. Let's look at each audience."

Kyle started with existing customers, and worked through each of the audience groups, explaining that the messages, and the vehicles that conveyed those messages, needed to achieve a clear, but different task. It ended up something like the following:

Existing customers	Shift from 'innovation and quality' to 'my innovation partner.'
Untroubled and unaware Manufacturing & Procurement	Get recognised as one of the players. No more and no less. Nothing about how we are different, just that we are in the pack. In fact, the more normal we look the better.
Untroubled and unaware Marketing & Sales	Create the need for a new list of partners in their mind. "Innovation partners" – allow other companies to be on the list also, (just make sure none of them make plastic beads).
Non-customers	As for *untroubled and unaware* Manufacturing and Procurement – get on the list.

"Now, let me confess something here. We commissioned some market research, and I sent you all a copy. You might remember that the key out-take from that was that we are positioned on innovation and quality, and the market wants reliability of supply.

"My confession is that I don't think reliability of supply is where we should position at all. That commits us to the commodity path and pricing, and we'll get caned. Our competitors commission research also, and it will tell them much the same thing. Let them go the reliability route, but let us move reliability to be something customers assume and not something anyone can get any traction with. We still have to deliver on reliability, but we talk a new message."

Brett briefly recounted his experience with Dairy Fresh during the week. Then, "I'm the first to agree. My guys can downplay reliability as something 'assumed', and introduce innovation as key. We just work it into the pitch and every conversation. Something like 'naturally, Mr Customer, reliability of supply is key. It always has been, and like all the major suppliers, we have that nailed. Let's though discuss what you need to achieve, rather than what you have the right to take for granted.'"

Wry smiles and raised eyebrows told Brett he had said something funny. Warren again broke the silence. "I think we are positioned." His answer indicated that they were impressed with Brett's ability, not amused by his humour.

Sarah stood up, and was unable to stifle a yawn despite her enthusiasm for their achievements. "A leg stretch. Back by 3.30, OK?"

Sarah had a decent break, and by 3.30 was ready to resume her role as facilitator and scribe. "Again folks, I'll be happy to summarise our discussions and circulate. Can we agree the key conclusions?" She wrote and talked and listed the following notes onto a sheet of butcher's paper.

– Of the three strategies, we adopted differentiation. This will mean we need to modify our product strategy for all customers, not just the *untroubled and unaware*.

– Our positioning challenge is to reposition with existing customers, get positioned basically for *untroubled and unaware* Manufacturing and the market generally, and create a new category into which we can be positioned for *untroubled and unaware* Sales and Marketing.

"Everyone OK with that? OK, I'll get it out tonight while it's fresh." And with that, the meeting concluded. It had been a good meeting.

From: Sarah Martin

Sent: Monday, 22 April

To: Sue Hunt
                  Graham Chase
                  Brett Marsden
                  Kyle Hoffman
                  Warren Jackson

Subject: Positioning

Hi all

I think this is what we agreed today. Email me with your corrections and I'll tidy up before next Monday.

Strategic positioning

We will position HardBits as a company with largely differentiated products for which customers will pay a premium. We have elected not to pursue a cost leadership or focus strategy.

We will command a premium relative to the rest of the market according to the value we add to our customers' efforts to innovate. We will spend less than this price premium, in our efforts to provide this differentiation. The difference will result in above industry average profits.

Market positioning

We will educate the market such that over time there is a new dimension that customers use to contrast their suppliers from each other. "Innovation partner" will come to mean "a partner who works with me to allow me to create innovative new products for my market."

For existing customers, we will achieve this by changing all our communication including grand things like the theming of our annual customer Christmas party, to minor things like the copy of our letters, invoices and email signatures. We will also change it materially by the behaviour and focus of our sales people and our engineers.

For Marketing and Sales Directors we consider to be prospects in our target audience, we will educate them about this new category, and seek to be in that category alongside their design, R&D and marketing partners. We will not help any direct competitors to enter this same category, endeavouring instead to include non-competitors in the way we describe the category.

We will achieve this category creation by selecting or recruiting appropriate sales people and skilling them in how to help Sales and Marketing Directors to use plastic to innovate. All our letters, web site copy, phone calls and other communication will reinforce the existence of this category of 'innovation partner' and our membership of that category.

Manufacturing Directors and their Procurement specialists within these same customers, plus the market more generally, will be reminded or advised of our membership of the existing category of plastics supplier.

Regards, Sarah

There was no doubt in Sue's mind that the team had a common cause, and were working well together. She allowed herself a short moment of self-congratulation as she drove home that night. *The week ahead had better pass fast,* she thought to herself, *because I can't wait until next Monday – we are going to build a real customer journey.*

A common problem

"But Brett, we were just too expensive. For the same product, EnviroPlas were 15% less than us, even after the discount you approved." John James had been with HardBits for five years, and was an old hand in the industry having worked for others for ten years before joining HardBits.

"But how can that be? We normally easily beat EnviroPlas on price." Brett suspected something else.

"Not in the 150 - 200 tonne range, Brett."

Brett lost patience. "Please..."

It turned out that John had been massively out-sold. EnviroPlas had provided the customer with a detailed Return on Investment calculator that showed when purchase, shipment, storage, and wastage were considered, they were cheapest. The 'hypothetical' quantity of 150 – 200 used in the calculator (cynically fixed to this quantity), invited the user to enter quoted prices from any potential supplier to do an 'apples for apples' comparison using the same quantity. Although this didn't necessarily reflect the customer's realistic requirement, it seemed a reasonable basis for the quotation. EnviroPlas' pricing model was stepped at various quantities (as were most), and this model just happened to coincide with the bottom of one of their steps.

"Sorry I'm late guys." Sue had shouted herself an extra-long run at the gym that morning and by the time she arrived the team was assembled and the coffees well underway.

"So, another big day I hope. Today we are going to build the client journey. Right from the start and I can hardly wait. We've done this in theory, but not in practice – it should be fun."

"Well, thanks Sue," said Warren. "Yes, we had a nice weekend, thanks. And you?"

"Oops, sorry. I hate being late, got a little frazzled. Please forgive my rudeness. All well then? Good, let's go Sarah." There were no flies on Sue.

Agenda

- Situation – what is going on in their world?
- Problem – what causes them pain?
- Need – what do they need to make this pain go away?
- Who most has this pain – do we have the target right?
- Who else can solve this – our competitors, non-competitors?
- Why will we win against these alternatives?
- What does their journey look like – the detail?

Situation

"So, what do we know about their world today?" Sarah asked of the team. "What is going on before the pain starts, that might lead to the pain?"

"Maybe I can kick off." This was an early start for Graham, more familiar to the team for his gifted, timely insights towards the end of play.

"Well, they are probably between 500 and 2000 employees. They have clear separation of responsibility between Manufacturing, Finance, Sales, and Marketing. They probably don't have a genuine R&D function – this is something more of a spare-time, in-the-basement type approach to new product development, or innovation generally. They have a range of products, mostly plastic or using significant amounts of it, use about 300 tonnes per annum of raw beads, negotiate contracts as often as two to three times per annum, and purchase with no warning and want it yesterday."

"For free," offered Brett.

Problem

"So, what is wrong with this?" asked Sarah, moving onto the next topic but hastily scribbling down some of Graham's key thoughts on the butcher's paper before passing two sheets to Warren who had offered to pin them up. "Remember, these are the *untroubled and unaware*, so they don't know they have a headache until it is a 'blinder'."

Brett had a go. "They get gazumped in the market by competitors who out-innovate them. They let their focus on material costs blind them to clever ways to address their total costs, and suffer margin pressure despite screwing all their suppliers and don't get why it happened. They suffer reputation damage and costs associated with product returns from retailers due to poor product quality or safety concerns."

Sarah was writing and gushing, "Wow," as she went. "Does that really happen?"

"I can tell you, these problems crop up all the time, and they tend to smack the company in the face when they least expect it."

"I protest." Sue had remained quiet until now. "We run the risk of assuming our customers are dumb; they are not. At DHM we were definitely a candidate for an innovation partner, but not because we could not do it ourselves. Our suppliers only focused on what their products did; none used their superior product knowledge to help us work out what could be done. I couldn't even get HardBits to ship in metric containers or send my statements on the correct day of month, let alone innovate with me. Let's be careful not to assume we are clever and they are not."

Brett knew better than to argue Sue down on this one, but felt her protest was politically correct, but unhelpful. "Sue, our sins notwithstanding, is that description of your problems at DHM correct any way?"

Sue reflected for a while before replying. "It's fine actually. I just want us to be mindful that our customers are smart, and we are yet to begin learning about their world."

Need

Sarah brought the discussion back on track. "So what do they need? What will make the problem go away?"

Brett again. "They think they need better quality raw materials at lower cost, but what they actually need is for their own products to improve, and for their processes to improve. And they need it to happen fast, yet they have limited resources."

Brett paused and changed his tone before recounting his meeting with John. He explained that a good sales person (or a good marketer – what a concession from Brett) could shape the customers' perception of their needs. "So what do we want at this point Sarah, what *they* think they need, or what *we* think they need? Who's to say which of us is right?"

Sue had already considered this. "I think it is *our* view of their need. Even though we are working on *their* journey, if we focus on a need that we don't want to be in the business of solving, then we are wasting our time. We can factor in a high leakage here to acknowledge that not all of them get to our version of the need, but we need them to need a need we can solve." Sue enjoyed her own tongue twister. "Phew. Try saying that fast ten times!"

Who most needs it?

Sarah wasn't going to let the momentum slip. "Who most has a need for fast, perhaps remedial innovation?"

"*Untroubled and unaware* Marketing Managers," offered Brett.

"Now, don't be lazy." It came out before Sarah thought about it, but Kyle's glance reminded her Brett was a Director and she was not, and she was here by invitation. "My apologies Brett. I had almost rehearsed that quip when I prepared for the meeting this morning. When I put 'who most needs it' on the agenda, I realised we have already covered this. I left it on the agenda to force us to think not so much about who we want to target, but to see if some crazy insight came from thinking about the need, and who would most be afflicted by it rather than…"

"It's OK Sarah, I was having a bit of fun." Brett felt no need to bring Sarah down. And then, speaking to Sarah but looking at Kyle, "You've earned your place here Sarah, take it easy. Seriously though, I think my answer holds. These are Marketing Managers, or Sales Managers too I suppose, who are not on top of their game. Frankly that's half of them in my view. Sorry Kyle, I don't mean you or your team, I'm thinking of some of our customers. There are some bright sparks, and some not-so-bright sparks."

"Brett, I'm going to have to repeat my cautionary note here." Sue felt the arrogance was misplaced and unhelpful. "Let's not assume they are not 'on their game.' The fact that they are untroubled and unaware is not a weakness, but a poor reflection on the plastics industry – we have not educated them well enough about the possibilities."

Brett ploughed on, obviously unmoved by Sue's case for the defence. "Anyway, Sales and Marketing Managers or Directors need innovation most, but maybe it's Manufacturing too. They are the ones who should be looking at quality and efficient operations don't you think Graham?"

"I do, but I liked our logic last week when we said that we should be talking *innovation* to Sales and Marketing, and *plastics* to Manufacturing. If we are not on their radar screen for plastic, we can't go talk to them about quality."

"So," Sarah was keen to nail this given her little dialogue with Brett. "Is that *really* who has the need?"

"It is Sarah. I get what you are doing, and maybe it's a good idea, but on this occasion, it just reinforced my belief that our target is the untroubled and unaware Marketing Manager."

Kyle couldn't help himself. "You're having too much fun with that picture Brett. I just have to remind you that we are also targeting untroubled and unaware Sales Managers."

"Sure."

Who else can meet the need?

"Just like the last topic," Sarah began, "I want to look at a question we have already covered, but from a different angle. Who else could meet this need for fast, perhaps remedial, innovation?"

"I think you've covered this in your previous note taking. Designers, external R&D, maybe more innovative job shops, marketing partners." Warren felt pleased to have something to contribute, even if it was only to remind them of past conclusions.

"No one else?" Sarah was less after additions, than confirmation that the team agreed. They did.

Why us?

"So why will we win? If we are only one of the sources of a solution to this need, and are not yet even on their radar screen at all, why will they choose us?"

"Well, sometimes they won't." Brett leaned forward, "But when they do, it'll be because of Graham's engineers. If they can come up with a good idea, they'll choose us."

Graham didn't agree. "I think a good designer should be just as capable of coming up with a novel idea as our engineers. What we can do better is come up with a plastic idea. We know plastic better than anyone, and we can come up with stronger, safer, more efficient, and more innovative ways to use plastic."

"But surely that means that sometimes we'll be competing with a steel solution, or other synthetics, paper or wood won't it?"

"Sure Brett, is that a problem?"

"No, I guess not. So we win because we know plastic better and can turn that knowledge to our customers' advantage."

Sue rose. "I think that's it." And then after a pause to see if there were any contrary views, "OK, have a stretch, and let's be back by 11.00. That'll give you a chance to clear any messages, but try not to get caught. We have a way to go."

Journey

Unlike the previous week, where everyone had been keen to avoid discussing the workshop over their break, today it was all they discussed. By the time they were ready to clear the coffee cups, they had convinced themselves that the journey was about right. They redrew the leaky funnel, but Brett insisted they replace the 'Position vendors' stage with 'Something happens.' "These guys aren't entertaining vendors. It's part of the reason why they are smacked in the side of the head by a problem."

Everything else remained the same.

"Let's recap then." Sarah wrote as she recounted their earlier discussions:

- Situation - 500-2000 employees, lack commitment to R&D. 300 tonnes/annum
- Problem - Out-innovated or product issues
- Need - Remedial innovation
- Who - *Untroubled and unaware* Marketing or Sales Directors
- Who else? - Design, external R&D, job shops or marketing partners
- Why us? - we know plastic
- Journey? - see paper

Graham stretched. It was almost lunch time and energy was low. "Sarah, I'm not comfortable with 'remedial innovation.' I know we've used it a few times today, but it is more than that. It's remedial if the problem surprises them. But sometimes we will make operational changes rather than product changes. Is it fair to say that they need product and process innovation?"

They agreed, and Sarah made the change.

- Need – Product and process innovation

"Well done guys, we get an early mark." Sue chirped. "See you all next Monday and we'll build lags and leakages. Kyle, Sarah, can you come back after 5 for about 15 minutes?"

From: Sarah Martin

Sent: Monday, 29 April

To: Sue Hunt
                Graham Chase
                Brett Marsden
                Kyle Hoffman
                Warren Jackson

Subject: Client Journey

See below for my recollection of what we agreed. As usual, your comments would be appreciated.

Situation

- 500-2000 employees,
- Lack an organisational commitment to R&D.
- Use approximately 300 tonnes/annum

Problem

- Out-innovated by competitors
- Costs blow out despite tight control on raw materials
- Reputation risk due to product quality or safety issues

Need

- Product innovation
- Process innovation

Who most has this need?

- *Untroubled and unaware* Marketing or Sales Directors

Who else can meet this need?

- Design
- External R&D
- Job shops
- Marketing partners

Why will we win?

— We know best how to turn plastic to our clients' advantage

What is the customer journey?

— Untroubled and unaware

— Something happens

— Acknowledge pain

— Define needs

— Receive proposals

— Select vendors

— Select single vendor

— Engage

Regards, Sarah

Despite generally being extremely happy with their progress, Sue felt uneasy about the buying process. She explained to Kyle and Sarah when they met later that afternoon that although it was she who was supposed to be the buyers' advocate at HardBits, she felt that the buyer's journey was an input, not an output. That is, they needed to build their own journey, one which ran parallel to the buyer's journey. Kyle took ownership for this and called a meeting with he, Brett and Sarah for Wednesday to work on it together.

Parallel journey

Kyle had to convince Brett that he wasn't trying to complicate a simple task. His example, borrowed from Sue, was telling.

"Once we are on the short-list, how many times do we get chosen by the recommender, only to get rejected by their boss?"

"Too often, why?"

"Well, it seems valid to have a stage about being selected as the single vendor, but you sort of have to do it twice don't you?"

"Well, no, the good guys cover all the bases simultaneously."

"How often does that really happen?"

"Not often enough. And sometimes we have the bases covered but our client still has to get his boss' OK."

They agreed that 'select single vendor' could be a two-step process. One by one they worked through each stage, and ended up with a table showing the parallel journeys. The two sides didn't align 100%. In part this was due to the addition of stages, and also because some stages were only valid for the buyer, and some only valid for the seller.

It needed some explanation. Even after agreeing the table with Brett, Kyle had to revisit the logic several times to remind himself why they had taken this path.

Their journey	Our journey
Untroubled and unaware	Find new names
	Position in category
Something happens	
Acknowledge pain	Identify problem
	Qualify and prioritise
	Establish credentials
Define needs	Define needs
Receive proposals	Propose solution
Select vendors	Prove concept
	Defeat competition
Select single vendor	Obtain management approval
Engage	Obtain contract
	Deliver
	Grow

To make clear that he was not advocating a change in the buyer-centricity of their model, Kyle created a table explaining the new proposed stages and for each stage, what the buyer was likely to be thinking at the completion of the stage.

Stage name	What do we want them to think when this stage concludes?
Find new names	This is an internal-only stage where targets are identified and profiled.
Position in category	*"You are one of the companies I recognise as members of this product category."*
Identify problem	*"I have a problem which members of this category can probably solve, and you seem to understand that problem."*
Qualify and prioritise	This is an internal-only stage where the leads generated are evaluated against some established criteria
Establish credentials	*"You are a credible provider in this product catgory and I understand something of your unique selling proposition."*
Define needs	*"I have a clearly defined need (problem or opportunity), and can articulate the payoff available to me for addressing this problem."*
Propose solution	*"I can see how your proposed solution might meet my needs and provide the payoff I seek."*
Prove concept	*"I can see how your proposed solution would work in my organisation, as outlined in your proposal."*
Defeat competition	*"Yours is the only solution I want to consider."*
Obtain management approval	*"My upline approvers and other stake-holders support my recommendation to accept your proposal."*
Obtain contract	*"You and I have a firm agreement binding us."*
Deliver	*"Your solution works as promised, and I am pleased."*
Grow	*"I have further needs I am interested in discussing with you."*

Kyle took the revised model around to each of the participants (Sue first of course), and gained their agreement to it before the week concluded. The Monday meeting would be a complete waste of time if they didn't all buy in to this fairly major change.

A model future

"So how does everyone feel about Kyle's parallel journey?"

"Actually, it's Brett's, Sarah's and mine Sue. We developed this together on Wednesday."

Brett explained further, "I helped build it, but I still have to remind myself why we have departed from the buying journey and have gone back to a selling journey. When I have to remind myself, I look at the *Establish credentials* stage. If we don't establish credentials, no prospect will be willing to discuss their needs with us. And if we are not at least seen by them as a member of the category, they won't see why they should discuss their problems with us, or let us suggest problems. Although we all persuaded ourselves of the merit of the buyer's journey, it is this parallel journey which described what *we* do. It is still crafted mindful of the buyer's journey, but is not exactly the same. So that is what I have to remind myself."

"Do you have these conversations with yourself often?" asked Warren.

"Yeah, all the time, thanks." They enjoyed Brett's discomfort for a second or two. Sarah reflected on how the cheap shots had been at her expense earlier in the process. She was pleased to no longer be the easy target.

"OK Ms Martin, the floor is yours." Sue seemed to enjoy the formality of this handover.

Lags & Leakages

They worked through the stages, allocating a realistic leakage and lag for each. Several times Sue or one of the others commented on the focus on failure (leakage) rather than success. They had agreed though, that it was a good discipline to think about how much would leak from the funnel at each stage. Thinking about how many they would lose in a given progression seemed to focus their attention somewhat more than was the case when they thought about how many they would successfully process through that same stage.

They agreed that they would start with 1000 prospects, and their aim was to produce revenues in line with the agreed objectives of securing 300 new customers over three years. Their lags and leakages all looked logical, defendable, and conservative.

Lag	Stage	Leakage
	Find New Names	
1	Position in Category	20%
1	Identify Problem	50%
1	Qualify & Prioritise	25%
4	Establish Credentials	70%
7	Define Need	25%
1	Propose Solution	5%
2	Prove Concept	25%
2	Defeat Competition	25%
1	Obtain Mgmt Approval	25%
1	Obtain Contract	25%
2	Deliver	1%
6	Grow	25%

Warren had ended up investing considerably more time than he had intended to build the model that could use these lags and leakages to predict future revenues.

The physical representation took no time at all, but the business logic and the algorithms were far more complex than he had imagined.

Warren kept cursing at himself every time IT told him they needed more resources. "Bloody lags." It turned out that Graham's little insight into the effect of lags had caused no end of problems. They had spent considerable time, and all they really had was a cobbled-together solution.

Anyway, the model had been built and was working. Now it was payback time. "Do you want the bad news or the really bad news?" Warren asked of anyone and everyone.

Brett wasn't in the mood for games. "So, what does that give us?"

"20 customers, all in the second quarter."

"What?" spluttered Brett. "So what's the really bad news?"

"Nothing after that, not a single sale. You're sacked, the lot of you." Warren paused to make sure he had the floor.

	Q1	Q2	Q3	Q4	Q5	Q6	Q7	Q8	Yr3	Total
Find New Names	1000									1000
Position in Category	800	0	0	0	0	0	0	0	0	800
Identify Problem	400	0	0	0	0	0	0	0	0	400
Qualify & Prioritise	300	0	0	0	0	0	0	0	0	300
Establish Credentials	90	0	0	0	0	0	0	0	0	90
Define Need	0	68	0	0	0	0	0	0	0	68
Propose Solution	0	64	0	0	0	0	0	0	0	64
Prove Concept	0	48	0	0	0	0	0	0	0	48
Defeat Competition	0	36	0	0	0	0	0	0	0	36
Obtain Mgmt Approval	0	27	0	0	0	0	0	0	0	27
Obtain Contract	0	20	0	0	0	0	0	0	0	20
Deliver	0	20	0	0	0	0	0	0	0	20
Grow	0	0	15	0	0	0	0	0	0	15

"A few points of reality though. One, it is rubbish to think we'll start all prospects at the top of the funnel all at once. You need to spread them out over at least a couple of quarters or your sales guys will go crazy for a quarter and then sit on their backsides for the rest of the three years. Two, we are assuming that once they've bought, they will never do so again. Three, we have not allowed for recycling. Four, we probably need more than 1000 prospects. Five, we are assuming we have zero momentum at the moment, and I assume we have some discussions already going on." He paused and enjoyed his moment of power.

Brett picked himself up off the floor. "OK, the only one of those we got right is the last one, because we actually do have zero momentum. We have no discussions going on with the *untroubled and unaware*. We are only talking to companies who already know they have a need. The other points I think we can work on. But together eh? Oh, and I think we've done ourselves an injustice. In truth we have two targets into each company, some will be more, but let's say two – the Sales Manager and the Marketing Manager. If we bomb with one, we can try the other, so we really have 2000 targets, not 1000."

And they did work on it together. Over and over again. Changing lags, leakages, recycling times, order values and nearly everything until they could take no more.

Warren had got over his power-junkie trip, and had been active in the debate about realistic success rates. And when they finally shut the models down for the night, having backed them up three times to be sure they didn't lose anything, he shared one last concern. "That is our best guess isn't it? I mean, we have no data to test our assumptions against, do we? It is all assumptions."

Brett was less concerned. "Of course they are assumptions. What do you think we use every time we build a business case? There are more assumptions with the leaky funnel, I'll grant you. But what we just built is the most robust model I've ever had of our predicted success in a market."

Brett was right, but Warren would have felt a whole lot more comfortable if they had benchmarks against which to test their assumptions.

Their final model showed the lags and leakages, and the number of successful progressions they anticipated each quarter, for each stage, over a three-year period. Their revenue almost matched their plan, although Graham had to concede that the ramp would be slower that he'd have liked. He feigned disgust at the "Bloody parabolic growth curves," but secretly thought it was about right.

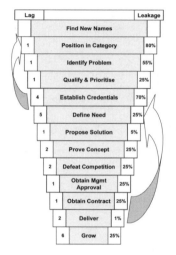

Lag	Stage	Leakage	Q1	Q2	Q3	Q4	Q5	Q6	Q7	Q8	Yr3	Total
	Find New Names		1000	1000								2000
1	Position in Category	80%	396	690	561	570	532	535	543	490	1859	6176
1	Identify Problem	55%	174	265	256	292	239	242	233	224	839	2763
1	Qualify & Prioritise	25%	129	198	190	204	180	187	170	172	630	2060
4	Establish Credentials	70%	20	58	58	57	63	53	54	51	191	605
5	Define Need	25%	15	34	66	88	102	115	111	115	445	1092
1	Propose Solution	5%	0	32	74	83	95	105	107	110	424	1030
2	Prove Concept	25%	0	24	44	60	77	75	80	81	319	761
2	Defeat Competition	25%	0	17	32	42	51	58	62	60	240	562
1	Obtain Mgmt Approval	25%	0	6	24	36	38	43	45	46	180	418
1	Obtain Contract	25%	0	5	17	26	29	32	33	34	135	311
2	Deliver	1%	0	5	16	22	28	32	33	34	134	304
6	Grow	25%	0	0	8	17	19	22	24	25	101	216

There were no follow up emails that night. Warren circulated the models on Wednesday without any comment. Just, "See you next Monday." This week's marathon effort had sapped all their energy.

They had learned that modelling seemed much easier than it turned out to be in reality, and that whilst intuitively they all knew it took a while to enter a new market and that losses (leakage) would be great, it was not until they allowed for a realistic leakage and lag for each stage that they realised how difficult the whole process of earning new customers really was.

Sue was no less flat than the others, and spent absolutely no time considering these matters or their learning for the balance of the week. It was not until Sunday night that she allowed herself to think about the week ahead. She didn't know what to feel about tomorrow. So she felt nothing, closed her eyes and was asleep in a flash.

Tactics

"Make mine a double would you Brett," mumbled Sue. Realising that if she felt this flat, the others must also, she started again. "Did anybody else feel washed out after our marathon on Monday?" Taking their expressions as affirmation, she smiled in understanding. "OK guys – let's remember how much we achieved."

This helped, and after the short debrief, they all felt a little better.

"So, before you start Sarah, just a couple of words to you all. I had thought about toning down the four anchors before showing them to the Board and then to you. They seemed a little harsh, especially the one about 'arbitrary tactics.' I decided not to tone them down for two reasons. Firstly, that is how I see it – the tactics *are* arbitrary, and secondly because it is not anyone's fault. I know we've been over this before, but I want to say it again.

"Current management science teaches us nothing about how to choose our tactics. There are whole forests killed every year to produce the many books on strategy, and there are more forests still on how to execute tactics well. But no one can show me anything which sensibly helps us select which tactics we need to execute if we want to effect the strategy. But I think we have that framework right in front of us today."

It was perhaps poor form to interrupt, but Kyle felt Sue was building her argument on a false assumption. He had to jump in. "Sue, forgive me for jumping in, but I must. I agree we have something new here, but it is operational, not strategic. Buyer behaviour is a fairly mature discipline. The issue is not that we have a new concept, but that we have a simple tool for taking the accepted science down to an operational level – a set of tactics."

Brett replied for Sue. "I buy that Kyle, but if buyer behaviour was so well understood, we wouldn't have had these discussions in the first place. I can give you countless examples of marketing tactics that are pretty groovy, but I'll bet London to a brick half of them won't withstand today's scrutiny. But because we are a new 'caring and sharing, wholly integrated' sales and marketing force, I'll give you a sales example of arbitrary tactics instead.

"Last week I had one of our better reps role-play the sales call in front of three new sales people. One of the new reps has been around a bit, and asked our old hand why she sent introductory letters then followed them up with a call, rather than the other way around. They looked at each other for a whole minute: the old hand could not believe why such a dumb question was being asked, and the new chum could not believe we did it that way. What they both showed is that they are a product of their past experience. Neither could defend their past approach, but both swore it was the only way to go."

Sue then resumed her point with the broader team. "Knowing the science requires one level of understanding. Being able to do something about it is not just an operational shift, but also a reflection of a deeper understanding. Whatever the case, we have a new way of looking at our tactics. Open minds, and, as importantly, a clean sheet of paper.

"Sarah, I want you to list all the tactics people ask about as we go along today, over there on the butcher's paper. Remember that our task is not to answer 'what are we going to do about tactic X?', but 'how can we achieve progression y?' We'll refer to the tactics list later as a checklist, but not as a starting point.

"So, Ms facilitator, your floor."

As good process-junkies, they began at the top, and worked their way down.

Find new names

They agreed to buy a one-time extract from a reputable database which listed manufacturers, filtered by industry and size. They would commission an outside research house (Kyle had one in mind) to call each company confirming their purchase quantities, current supplier, and contact details for Sales & Marketing Directors. Kyle believed that if they used outside field workers, the research house could get it done within a month as he had discussed similar work with the research house previously.

Position in category

"So, we could send these prospects a direct mail piece, advertise, call them up, send them a letter, whatever. What do we actually *want* to do?" Sarah was happy to leave the answers to this to Kyle and Brett.

"I'm a bit confused Sarah. Aren't these two the same?" Brett asked pointing to 'position in category' and 'identify problem.' "Wouldn't we go straight to getting them to identify a problem?"

They discussed this for a while, before Graham produced one of his gems. "I'm no marketer, but I think what we are seeing here is confusion between success and failure." He paused, got no reaction, so continued. "If we try to answer the question 'what do we need to do to achieve successful progression at stage three?' then we get one answer. If we ask 'what if we try to achieve successful progression at stage 4 and fail, what can we assume was locked in from our successful progression at stage 3?' we get a different answer." Again, no reaction, so he continued.

"For example, let's say we try to get a prospect to identify that they have a problem. Maybe we send them a letter and spell out the three most common problems, and ask them 'do you have any of these problems?' If they say 'yes', we have succeeded. If they say 'no', then we have failed. But this is good failure, because at least we are registered in their mind as someone who is interested in solving such and such a problem."

"So what does bad failure look like?" Brett wasn't being sarcastic. He had learned to hear Graham out.

"Bad failure is the letter gets thrown in the bin. We didn't get them to identify the problem, and we didn't get to fall back to at least being positioned in their mind."

Sarah enjoyed having Graham in the driver's seat rather than her for a change. "So what do we actually do in each stage?"

"We try at each stage to earn the right to enter the next stage. But we do it in a way that if we fail, we meet at least the objectives of the stage we are in." Graham sat down again, indicating he was done.

Sarah resumed her feet, and without fully understanding what Graham had just said or where it would take them, agreed to give it a go. They built and rebuilt the tactics until they could identify no further changes, or they were tired, or both. Sarah suspected the table they produced would be changed many times before they really called it complete, but this was not a bad start.

Find new names	Buy database. Filter. Research house to build profiles and contact details.
Position in category	Letter outlining common problems.
Identify problem	Call to seek meeting, and gain agreement that the problem exists.
Qualify and prioritise	Do they meet the profile, and are they concerned enough about the problem?
Establish credentials	Meeting. 5 min desktop presentation of credentials, then SPIN questions leading to need.
Define needs	Meeting. SPIN questions incl. payoff, and purchase parameters.
Propose solution	Boilerplate proposal customised to their needs and payoff. Propose pilot.
Prove concept	Proof of concept pilot, costed into first stage only if they proceed.
Defeat competition	Workshop agreement from sponsor & other stakeholders to decision criteria.
Obtain management approval	Arrange single 'peer' meeting between highest decision maker from client, and counterpart Director at HardBits.
Obtain contract	Submit draft agreements at time of proof of concept, and request client legal to review early.
Deliver	Hold review meetings with sponsor weekly x 4, fortnightly x 4, then monthly.
Grow	Close each meeting with open question. "How else can we help you?"

Good enough tactics

Sue was less confident they had the tactics right. "So, Brett. If we sent a letter and followed it up with a call, and culled a few we didn't think were worried enough, would that get us face to face with 605 new prospects?"

"Over three years, sure. That's one in four, which is high, but if we get to keep trying, sure, I can get that now from the guys pretty much."

Sue continued. "What if I asked that again? Can you get face to face with 605 new prospects who are deeply worried about one of the three problems that you have expressly asked them to acknowledge their concern about?"

"Ah, now I get you. You know what, I still say these tactics will get us there, but I wouldn't say that's what we do today. In fact, it's not."

"So, would you expect to be able to achieve more out of 605 face to face meetings this way, than what we do today?"

Brett sensed himself being backed into a corner, but didn't fight it. "Yes, but we have that factored already here. We are planning to submit 1030 proposals to these 605. I understand from last week that this includes those who we meet with, fail to connect with, but try again at some later stage. Right now, I'd guess we are lucky to get 250 proposals out of 500 first time meetings. 1030 is a big improvement.

"So," Sue was unrelenting "Are our tactics good enough to get us 1030 proposal opportunities out of 605 first meetings over three years?"

"Jeez Sue, I don't know. You know, we have never had to test ourselves so rigorously. I just don't know." This was the most honest Sue had ever seen Brett; he was not one to admit he didn't have the answers. He continued, "What I do know, is that the way we do it today is to say 'forecast is looking flat, we need some more leads' and then fly off at Marketing for not giving us enough leads. At least this way I know exactly what we need to achieve.

"I think, Sue, that you've got to give us some time to test our proposed tactics before we can say they are good enough."

Brett was right, and Sue backed down. For the first time, she had a framework for getting things right, and was impatient to extract the maximum out of it, and all those using it. But Sue didn't need to alienate Brett or the others. This was a tool for them as well as for her.

Recycling

Sarah broke the silence. "Sue, before we go too far down that path, we need also to look at how we can incubate our leaked prospects from the top of the funnel, and nurture our leakage from the bottom half."

The team had come to refer to the strategies for warming up their leaked prospects as 'incubation' and 'nurturing' to differentiate between the relatively light touch they would invest in their early failures compared to the heavier investment they would make in prospects who had progressed further and failed at one of the later stages.

Sarah continued. "Just in case you are thinking we can let ourselves off the hook here, get this: We have 2000 prospects, and only 304 of them become customers. All our work on tactics today has been about these 304, but what are we going to do about the 1696 that don't become customers?"

Warren was busy punching into his calculator, and was ready to have some fun. "It's worse than that Sarah, if we don't recycle, we'll get only 7% of the customers that have already been qualified, which by the way is less than half a percent of those who enter the funnel. We go from 7% to 15% success with qualified prospects only because we recycle."

The maths was lost on all except Warren at this stage, but they were willing to accept Sarah's original point that they needed recycling strategies.

A plan

The team went on to develop their incubation and nurturing strategies, to refine their in-funnel strategies, and even to develop some early thoughts about how they would measure actual progression through the funnel. They realised that measurement of progress would allow them to know if they were on target or not, far earlier than their sales forecast did, and would also allow them to track the success of individual tactics.

Sarah offered to dissect their planned tactics and to build a plan showing which tactics needed some set up work, and which needed constant use. They adopted the term 'rhythm' to describe tactics which required repeated use, because it connoted a sense of momentum, rather than the stop/start nature of many of their past activities.

When Sarah called the meeting to a close at 6pm, Sue was asked if she would like a copy of the final plan. The plan Sue finally signed off on is contained as an appendix to this book.

Sue realised that this workshop was the turning point. They were now at a point where she would perhaps become less of an asset to their planning. The subtleties of the funnel were no longer hers to identify, sell or to control.

The leaky funnel didn't belong to Sue. It belonged to HardBits and to the team that created it.

Rhythm

September

"A bit of news guys. I'm leaving."

Everyone except Graham looked up, shocked.

"It's OK. I'm not leaving you, and I'm not leaving HardBits, but I am leaving this war room. You have achieved an incredible amount. When we agreed the plan back in early May, we had only seven weeks to prepare all the tactics for the July launch. We expected then, that three months into the execution of your acquisition program you would not yet have any customers, but would have had 36 first-time meetings. We're now three months into execution, and have conducted a little short of 30 first-time meetings, but already we have seven new customers from those 30. We're ahead of plan and I have no doubt you are going to remain well ahead of plan.

"Importantly for me though, you have helped reshape Hard-Bits into a company worthy of the endorsement of those seven new customers. We have walked a mile (well maybe 1000 miles) in the shoes of our customers and prospects, and have learned how to earn the right to walk 1000 more. We are doing this with fewer resources, and we are not busting a boiler. This is sustainable growth.

"The four anchors have been well and truly addressed.

"I have been here almost 12 months, and have learned to respect you each for your differences, for your similarities, and for your commitment.

"Our next challenge is to learn how to be efficient at meeting this increased demand. Manufacturing and Operations is coping well right now, but will undoubtedly become an issue for us within the quarter. Graham has invited me to spend more time with him working out how we can acquire additional capacity. I can tell you I am more nervous about going into Graham's world, than I ever was playing a part in building a new approach to earning customers.

"Naturally, Graham will also be leaving this forum with me, and I think it's time for you to let Warren off the hook too. You'll need to call on Graham and Warren, and me for that matter, from time to time, and I am sure we'd all welcome the invitation. I'll expect frequent reports on progress, of course.

"I won't drone on for long, but I do want to remind you of what has changed over the last 12 months. There are four major changes that deserve highlighting:

1. We have refocused the whole marketing and sales force around the way our customers buy.
2. We have the whole sales and marketing process modelled to within an inch of its life and can now accurately determine whether a 5% improvement in one stage would have a greater impact than 5% in another, or whether greater gain would be obtained from shortening the time it takes us for a stage.
3. We are now able to accurately benchmark our granular success rates internally as well as against other companies.
4. We have stopped many of our old sales and marketing initiatives and started a few, but those we kept are now earning their keep."

"These are big changes and we are seeing some great results.

"Sarah, the funnel is yours to evolve. Write that book if you will, but Kyle and I have a request of you, which might keep you busy for the next little while. We'd like to move your office onto the eighth floor, along with my other direct-reports, if that suits."

Sarah glanced at Kyle, not quite sure of what she had just heard. "Congratulations Sarah," said Kyle, answering Sarah's implied question. "Sue and I feel that Strategy and Planning is now a force equal to Marketing and Sales, and we'd welcome you as a peer. Officially that is, because you've been driving us nuts for months anyway."

Helen rolled a trolley into the room with a large cake and a bottle of Champagne. "Turn off that silly espresso machine and help me open this bubbly. You lot need to drink less coffee anyway."

Sarah's cup was overflowing, Sue's funnel was leaking, and Helen's espresso machine had stopped shooting steam. Somehow this seemed about right.

Come Monday

Sue's journey had taken fully twelve months, had started slowly, and had initially been without any real sense of purpose. Along the way, she had taken more blind alleys than productive ones, and had learned as many lessons she would rather forget as those she wished to retain.

The Board meeting to be held later that afternoon was troubling Sue. She had been so close to the development of the new plan with her team that she worried that perhaps it would look a little 'over-cooked', and that her lack of objectivity would be apparent to the other Directors. It was too late to do anything now though, as they all had a copy of the plan and progress report for reading before the Board meeting.

Importantly for Sue, she felt that this first journey was now complete, and she would need the Board's support for the next stage – working with Graham on acquiring additional manufacturing capacity.

As much for her own clarity, as for those who followed her, Sue set out to summarise what she would do if she were again attempting to improve the effectiveness of the company's efforts to earn more customers.

1 – Accept reality

Gain agreement from the key stakeholders (usually Sales, Marketing, Finance, and Operations) that in even the best run companies, the customer acquisition process is less effective than it could be, and that they lack credible data to know how good or bad they really are.

2 – Understand the buyer's journey

Most of us understand our customers pretty well, but do we understand how they buy? Again, probably reasonably well. The issue is that we haven't tested this understanding of their process, and don't know whether it incorporates all the stages they go through along the way to identifying a need, or if the journey starts with a need already in mind.

3 – Dimension the journey

Before we changed our approach to planning we knew what our conversion rates were in terms of what percentage of proposals were accepted, but we didn't break it down, and certainly didn't dimension the whole journey. We now know we need to dimension the buyer's journey in its entirety, and that we have to know at least the lag, leakage, and recycling rates for each stage in the journey.

4 - Select strategies and tactics for each stage of the journey

Before, we used to select a mix of strategies and tactics for Marketing and another list for Sales, and expect this mix to deliver a result. But we didn't know which tactic was contributing well and which was not. Now we select them for their specific contribution to a single stage of the buyer's journey, and stress-test them to be sure they are a good enough mix of strategies and tactics to achieve *that* journey progression at *that* rate of success over *that* period of time. It's hard, but it makes a huge difference.

5 - Measure and benchmark

Because the previous step in this process gives us something so concrete to shoot for, we now measure our prospect progression for every stage in their journey. We know, for example, whether we are likely to run into strife three months down the track because we are short of prospects at the earlier stages of the journey. And we benchmark ourselves: division against division, sales team against sales team, and hope eventually to benchmark externally, so we know which aspects we are better at than others, and which need some work.

Whilst writing this down had perhaps been a useful process, Sue knew this was far too much detail and too academic for the Board. They would want to know only what had changed, and whether this was going to deliver a result. Her summary slide was far more effective.

Outputs

- Sales and Marketing are on the same page – the customer's
- We know exactly:
    - what we have to do,
    - in what quantity and
    - why
- We are now benchmarking our effectiveness
    - internally now
    - externally later
- We are spending less (stopped many low-yield activities)
- We won seven new customers this quarter

"This is rather pleasant." Lars' delight at the changed location for the Board meeting shouldn't have come as a surprise. It was his idea to get the Directors off site after all.

The view over the bay was pretty spectacular though, and the afternoon sunlight gave the waves a depth of colour that seemed somehow to penetrate the tall glass windows of *The Catalina* restaurant and into the meeting room they had hired for the afternoon.

The mood of the meeting was more impacted by their collective sense of achievement, but the environment perhaps added something of a sense of occasion. The operational aspects of the meeting were nonetheless as brief as always, and Sue's single summary slide was all that was needed to cap the discussion about their new plan for earning new customers.

"OK. So what now Sue?" Lars knew of Graham and Sue's plans to increase capacity, and had received Graham's report recommending acquisition of a small operator for short-run manufacturing to help their customers innovate.

The seven wins had been earned without the need to offer this capability, but their dialogue with customers and prospects had confirmed that this was still a valid strategy. Graham put his argument forcefully and with characteristic clarity.

Like Frank McInroth before them however, Sue and Graham lost their case to purchase this small unprofitable manufacturer, but unlike in Frank's case, this time the baby didn't go out with the bath water. Lars countered Graham's recommendation with one of his own, which involved building additional manufacturing capacity plus the ability for short-run manufacture into a single site. His argument about the ability to showcase their flexible manufacturing operation to prospective customers left little room for debate, and he had already lined up provisional funding.

With clearly no point in fighting (save it for the ones you can win), Sue's gaze drifted through the windows of *The Catalina* and out to the bay. As her focus adjusted to the view through the sea-salt affected windows, she watched as the crew of *Four Seasons* weighed anchor and headed out for a late afternoon sail.

Appendices

1 - HardBits' plan for earning new customers

Prepared by:

Sarah Martin
Kyle Hoffman
Brett Marsden
Warren Jackson
Graham Chase
Sue Hunt

Strategy

To whom?

We will target the Marketing and Sales Directors of the 1000 companies who are currently using plastics as a key component of their product development, but lack the ability to innovate substantially in house.

Through whom?

We will use our Marketing team to profile the above companies, (including name and all contact details), then to warm these prospects before Sales' involvement. Our direct sales force will be trained to identify defined needs from these prospects and to bring a deal to the table. Sales will own closure, but we expect the broader organisation to be involved in an innovation sale.

With what?

Our standard product, together with a product innovation team, and a yet-to-be-acquired short-run facility will be packaged as a new product innovation partnership. Pricing will be set individually for each company based on the value we believe they will gain from this innovation, but will be no less than base price + 20%.

Competitive strategy

5 is strongest 1 is weakest	HardBits	Plastix	GRM	EnviroPlas	EuroNue	Sartle	Average
Reputation as an innovator	4	2	1	3	2	2	2.3
Ability to assist new development	2	3	2	2	3	3	2.5
Competitive base product	3	4	3	2	2	1	2.5
Ability to engage with the buyer	2	3	2	4	3	2	2.7
Capacity to serve new market	3	3	2	2	2	4	2.7
Total	14	15	10	13	12	12	13

HardBits is positioned as an innovator, but lacks the ability to assist new customers to innovate. We will form an innovation team from Manufacturing, and acquire some capability to produce short runs necessary for product innovation.

We will move past our competition. That is, we will seek to create our own position and not position off other vendors. We will not engage in competitive knock offs, but will retrain our sales force to set an agenda with prospects that leaves them only one option – HardBits.

Strategic positioning

Broad	Cost leadership	**Differentiation**
Narrow	Focus	

We will command a premium relative to the rest of the market because of the value we add to our customers' efforts to innovate. We will spend less than this price premium in our efforts to provide this differentiation. The difference will result in above industry average profits.

Objectives

The effect of this new business drive will be to grow 20% revenues cumulative for three years before flattening out.

		New clients gained	New customers cumulative	Volume per client (tonnes)	New volume sold (tonnes)	Volume cumulative (tonnes)	Current volume sold (tonnes)	Price per tonne (A$)	Revenue (A$'000)
Year 1	Q1	0	0	300	0	0	10,000	$2,500	$25,000
	Q2	14	14	300	4,200	4,200	10,000	$2,500	$35,500
	Q3	16	30	300	4,800	9,000	10,000	$2,500	$37,000
	Q4	19	49	300	5,700	14,700	10,000	$2,500	$39,250
Year 2	Q1	21	70	300	6,300	21,000	10,000	$2,500	$40,750
	Q2	24	94	300	7,200	28,200	10,000	$2,500	$43,000
	Q3	28	122	300	8,400	36,600	10,000	$2,500	$46,000
	Q4	32	154	300	9,600	46,200	10,000	$2,500	$49,000
Year 3	Q1-4	146	300	300	43,800	90,000	40,000	$2,500	$209,500

Market positioning

We will educate the market to create a new dimension customers use to contrast their suppliers from each other. 'Innovation partner' will come to mean 'a partner who works with me to allow me to create innovative new products for my market.'

For existing customers, we will achieve this by changing all our communication including everything from theming of our annual customer Christmas party, to minor things like the copy of our letters, invoices and email signatures. We will also change it by the behaviour and focus of our sales people and our engineers.

For Marketing and Sales Directors we consider to be prospects in our target audience, we will educate them about this new category, and seek to be in that category alongside their design, R&D

and marketing partners. We will not allow any direct competitors to enter this same category. We will achieve this category creation by selecting or recruiting appropriate sales people and skilling them in how to help Sales and Marketing Directors to use plastic to innovate. All our letters, web site copy, phone calls and other communication will reinforce the existence of this category of 'innovation partner' and our membership of that category.

Manufacturing Directors and their procurement specialists within these same customers, plus the market more generally, will be reminded or advised of our membership of the existing category of plastics supplier. This will be achieved through broad promotional tactics such as advertising, PR, trade show attendance, etcetera.

A journey through problems

Situation

Manufacturers with between 500 and 2000 employees, and use approximately 300 tonnes/annum. They lack an organisational commitment to R&D and recognise this.

Problem

Their lack of R&D capability means that they are often out-innovated by competitors. Despite a tight control on raw materials, their costs blow out due to inefficiencies relative to their competition, brought about by their lack of investment in efficient new processes and infrastructure. They face reputation risk due to product quality or safety issues for the same reasons.

Need

They need to create new products, and need to improve their processes for current products.

Who most has this need?

Marketing or Sales Directors in manufacturers without a meaningful commitment to R&D.

Who else can meet this need?

- Design companies
- External R&D
- Job shops
- Marketing partners

Why will we win?

We will leverage our superior knowledge of plastic and the way it can be used in the manufacturing process.

Progression matrix

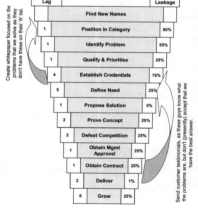

	Q1	Q2	Q3	Q4	Q5	Q6	Q7	Q8	Yr3	Total
Find New Names	1000	1000								2000
Position in Category	396	690	561	570	532	535	543	490	1859	6176
Identify Problem	174	265	256	292	239	242	233	224	839	2763
Qualify & Prioritise	129	198	190	204	180	187	170	172	630	2060
Establish Credentials	20	58	58	57	63	53	54	51	191	605
Define Need	15	34	66	88	102	115	111	115	445	1092
Propose Solution	0	32	74	83	95	105	107	110	424	1030
Prove Concept	0	24	44	60	77	75	80	81	319	761
Defeat Competition	0	17	32	42	51	58	62	60	240	562
Obtain Mgmt Approval	0	6	24	36	38	43	45	46	180	418
Obtain Contract	0	5	17	26	29	32	33	34	135	311
Deliver	0	5	16	22	28	32	33	34	134	304
Grow	0	0	8	17	19	22	24	25	101	216

Progression plan

Find new names	Buy database. Filter. Research house to build profiles and contact details.
Position in category	Letter outlining common problems.
Identify problem	Call to seek meeting, and gain agreement that the problem exists.
Qualify and prioritise	Do they meet the profile, and are they concerned enough about the problem?
Establish credentials	Meeting. 5 min desktop presentation of credentials, then SPIN questions leading to need.
Define needs	Meeting. SPIN questions incl. payoff, and purchase parameters.
Propose solution	Boilerplate proposal customised to their needs and payoff. Propose pilot.
Prove concept	Proof of concept pilot, costed into first stage only if they proceed.
Defeat competition	Workshop agreement from sponsor & other stakeholders to decision criteria.
Obtain management approval	Arrange single 'peer' meeting between highest decision maker from client, and counterpart Director at HardBits.
Obtain contract	Submit draft agreements at time of proof of concept, and request client legal to review early.
Deliver	Hold review meetings with sponsor weekly x 4, fortnightly x 4, then monthly.
Grow	Close each meeting with open question. "How else can we help you?"

Plan

Jul	Aug	Sep
− Purchase initial 1000 names − Engage research house to build profiles of companies from database	− Build plan for first approach − Build plan for first meeting including SPIN questions to acknowledge problem − Qualification matrix − Approach 200 prospects	− Build credentials presentation − Build templates (approach letters, follow up letters / emails, proposal) − Approach 196 prospects − Hold 20 first time presentations
Q2	**Q3**	**Q4**
− Purchase additional 1000 names − Series of white-papers on the problems to "incubate" all leaked early-funnel prospects − Approach 690 prospects − Hold 58 first presentations − Submit 32 proposals − Close 5 new deals	− Series of customer testimonials to 'nurture' all leaked late-funnel prospects − Approach 561 prospects − Hold 58 first presentations − Submit 74 proposals − Close 17 new deals	− Approach 570 prospects − Hold 57 first presentations − Submit 83 proposals − Close 26 new deals

Yr 2
− Approach 2099 prospects − Hold 221 first presentations − Submit 416 proposals − Close 128 new deals

2 - HardBits' key players

HardBits' Board of Management

HardBits' Executive Team

3 - Sue's library

The Leaky Funnel was inspired by many original thinkers. The books below are those that most influenced us (and therefore Sue and her team). They are presented in the order in which they appear in Sue's journey.

SPIN Selling

Neil Rackham. McGraw-Hill Inc., USA, 1988.

Business libraries and book stores are littered with texts on sales management. Published in 1988, this is still the one that will most impact your immediate success. *SPIN Selling* draws on over 35,000 interviews with sales people, or observations of them in the field, and concludes that good sales people build needs and poor sales people pitch products. You'll see influences of *SPIN Selling* in MathMarketing's approach to improving sales and marketing effectiveness.

(*SPIN* is a registered trademark of Huthwaite, Inc.)

A New Brand World: Eight Principles for Achieving Brand Leadership in the 21st Century

Scott Bedbury, and Stephen Fenichell (Contributor). Viking Press, USA, 2002

His major role in the development of two great global brands – Nike and Starbucks – says enough. Although the positioning chapter in *Kellogg on Marketing* explains why many teachings which are exclusively drawn from consumer markets don't hold in business markets, it is a brave marketer who completely ignores the experience of a senior marketing executive with runs on the board like Fenichell.

Rethinking The Sales Force: Redefining Selling to Create and Capture Customer Value

Neil Rackham and John DeVincentis. The McGraw-Hill Companies, Inc., USA, 1999.

Although somewhat less impactful (for us) than Rackham's first book *SPIN Selling*, in *Rethinking the Sales Force*, Rackham and DeVincentis point out that sales forces are often structured around conveniences for the vendor rather than the buying style of the customer. They offer a simple, usable framework to deal with the three types of buyer: *intrinsic* (their value comes from the product alone), *extrinsic* (their value comes from the way the product is applied), and *strategic* (they want to create new value by aligning their resources with yours).

Positioning: The Battle for Your Mind

Al Ries, and Jack Trout. McGraw-Hill Inc., New York, NY, USA, 1981

Although *Kellogg on Marketing* (see later) provides a framework for positioning that we find more usable (especially in business-to-business marketing), Ries and Trout were the pioneers of positioning, and a full appreciation of this not-so-subtle art is enhanced by knowing its origins.

Competitive Strategy: Techniques for Analyzing Industries and Competitors

Michael Porter. The Free Press, Simon & Schuster Inc., USA, 1980.

25 years after first being published, the framework for understanding profitability detailed in *Competitive Strategy* holds as valid today. Porter explains why those generating more profit than their

rivals in any given industry hold to any *one* of three strategies: cost leadership (not price), focus or differentiation. It is heavy going, but well worth reading and rereading.

Kellogg on Marketing

Dawn Iacobucci (editor). John Wiley & Sons, Inc., USA, 2001.

Alice M Tybout and Brian Sternthal from Kellogg University strip the 'fluff' from market positioning to leave a believable and usable core. They explain that efforts to position a brand are usually around communicating its point of difference, but that this doesn't 'stick' if the brand is not already firmly positioned within the product category. For brands yet to hold such a position, marketers should instead communicate the brand's similarities with established members. Seemingly academic, this is a simple revelation, and explains why so often positioning efforts for new brands fail.

Permission Marketing: Turning Strangers Into Friends, and Friends Into Customers

Seth Godin. Simon & Schuster Inc., USA, 1999.

As a pioneer of effective email marketing, Seth Goddin introduced a novel idea in this popular book: most of our marketing is interrupting our audience. Ineffective advertising and offensive SPAM are not markedly different from each other, in that at best they miss the point, or perhaps more likely, they evidence how much the seller is willing to ignore they buyer. Goddin gives great examples of unwelcome interruption, and encourages the reader to build a permission-based dialogue with their market.

The Buck Starts Here: Profit-Based Sales & Marketing Made Easy

Mary & Michael Molloy. Pinnaflex Educational Resources, Inc; Cincinnati, Ohio, USA, 1999

In an effusive and compelling manner, Mary and Michael Molloy lead us to a practical understanding of a simple means to determine the ROI of sales and marketing options.

Inside the Tornado: Marketing Strategies From Silicon Valley's Cutting Edge

Geoffrey Moore. HarperCollins Publishers, Inc., New York, NY, USA, 1995.

An excellent insight into the macro strategy settings needed by a business as its prospective customers move from scepticism to active enthusiasm. It also contains an adequate summary of *Crossing the Chasm* (Moore's first book), which describes the macro strategy settings needed by a business after it has picked the low-hanging fruit of an early market.

For:

- further information on sales and marketing effectiveness,
- crisp reviews of books we have found to be useful on the subject of sales and marketing effectiveness, and
- a free web-based tool to help you dimension a basic sales funnel

visit www.leakyfunnel.com

Notes

Notes

Notes

Notes

Notes

Notes

Notes

Notes

About the author

Hugh Macfarlane has learned from and provided advice to some extraordinary individuals over the last 20 years. They have been investors, Boards, CEOs, Directors of Sales or Marketing, and other senior managers of global and local corporations leading in their fields of computer hardware and software, telecommunications, healthcare and financial services. Their businesses market products and services with sales cycles ranging from short and highly transactional, to long, complex and strategic.

The central argument of *The Leaky Funnel*, that a new framework is needed for planning and managing the aggregate Sales and Marketing force, is based on many years of experience serving these leaders. The new framework proposed in the book has now been well proven by many leading global and local businesses as a means of accelerating the effectiveness of their endeavours to earn more customers.